FINE ARTS, MUSIC AND LITERATURE

WHAT YOUR EYES TELL YOUR BRAIN ABOUT ART

INSIGHTS FROM NEUROAESTHETICS AND SCANPATH EYE MOVEMENTS

FINE ARTS, MUSIC AND LITERATURE

Additional books in this series can be found on Nova's website
under the Series tab.

Additional e-books in this series can be found on Nova's website
under the eBooks tab.

FINE ARTS, MUSIC AND LITERATURE

WHAT YOUR EYES TELL YOUR BRAIN ABOUT ART

INSIGHTS FROM NEUROAESTHETICS AND SCANPATH EYE MOVEMENTS

WOLFGANG H. ZANGEMEISTER

AND

CLAUDIO M. PRIVITERA

nova
science publishers
New York

NOTICE TO THE READER

Library of Congress Cataloging-in-Publication Data

ISBN: 978-1-53612-435-4

Published by Nova Science Publishers, Inc. † New York

to Leopold

to Michela

CONTENTS

PREFACE

In the last decade, we have observed a continuous increase of interest in eye movements research. According to a recent investigation (*Editorial by Becker, Horstmann and Herwig published in 2014 in J. Ophthalmology*) eye movements are discussed in over one million publications. The number of publications with eye movement in the title or abstract has been steadily increasing over the years - as shown in Figure 1 of this editorial. About 1,200 papers were published in 2013. The last decade has also witnessed the emergence of many new sub-disciplines in the field of neuroscience and cognition – one is *neuroaesthetics* which refers to the (neuro-) science of aesthetic perception of art.

The title and contents of our book have been inspired by a very influential research article.[1] It is one of the most cited scientific papers of all time, published in 1959 by a team of neurophysiologists and engineers, Lettvin, McCulloch and Pitts who are considered to be the founders of modern cybernetics. Their article, "What the Frog's Eye Tells the Frog's Brain" refers to the role of internal cortical models in the communication or interfacing of the information in the outside world with the practical

---

[1] In the cover: Bonnard's "After the meal" (1925). A woman in the upper left-hand corner seems like entering the scene in a blurry and low contrast patch of colors. Arrows, showing the flow of the extended eye movements, support late emotional response which was one of the artist's artistic and perceptual objective

contextual task of the viewer. It shows how eye movements are the modality of this communication. The same duality between eye movements and internal models plays a fundamental role in humans. When we look, e.g., at art, it explains those neurological processes involved in neuroaesthetics. Our book undertakes this innovative approach to neuroaesthetics. It explains this duality and discusses the communication between the artist and the viewer's aesthetic perception. Our experience on Scanpath eye movements and neuroaesthetics (see appended reference selected list of our publications) demonstrates our interest and knowledge on this fascinating subject. It originated from our collaboration with the late Larry Stark, who pioneered the modern studies on eye movements and defined the Scanpath Theory. This book had not been possible without his seminal and inspiring contribution to the domain.

The book is structured into five chapters.

Chapter 1 serves as an introduction to fundamental notions – the neurology of aesthetics. It is about the idea of art as a form of communication, and explains perception as an active matching between a "Top" (the viewer's mind) and a "Down" (the viewer's sensorial machinery), and at last the very deep philosophical quandary of what is beauty in art.

Chapter 2 is about Eye Movements and the Scanpath Theory of vision perception. It discusses the role of visual attention for controlling active vision, the meaning of mental binding and the analysis of Eye Movements as the key to understanding aesthetic processes.

Chapter 3 introduces Claude Shannon's Information Theory using it as a matrix into which to embed the Top-Down active vision Scanpath Theory. We explain the main concept of neuroaesthetics as a form of communication: With the artist being the sender, the viewer the receiver. The sequence of eye fixations (and corresponding foveations) is the dynamic channel through which the communication is implemented in vision.

Chapter 4 discusses art critique: The role of the viewer's training and expectation, the dilemma of the aesthetics of art versus non-art and how all this affects the viewing mode.

Finally, Chapter 5 treats the intimacy of the artistic process, showing the unique implementation of the communicative experience between the artist and the viewer – the relation between a pictorial representation defined by the artist and modes of AWE generated in the viewer during active looking. Since we want non-scientists to read and appreciate the book, we have tried to keep the language and the notes on special results of neuroscience easy and understandable with limited scientific terminology. The only advised prerequisites to reading and enjoying this book are an interest in art and the brain. Our intended readership thus comprehends a wide range of scholars or professionals including graduate students and interested laymen in, i) our field, ii) disciplines other than our own fields, like psychology, art critique and history, iii) aesthetics and art philosophy.

ABOUT THE AUTHORS

Wolfgang H. Zangemeister studied medicine in Berlin and Munich, where he took his medical examination in 1971. He was promoted to Dr. med. at the Max-Planck-Institute for Psychiatry in Munich in the lab of Norbert Mattussek in 1972 at the Ludwig-Maximilians-University of Munich.

Zangemeister also studied painting and kinetic sculpture at the Academy of Fine Arts Munich from October 1967 to July 1971 where he attended the class of Mac Zimmermann. In July 1971, he presented with his group "Fiction Munich" a kinetic environment at the exhibition "Young German art: 14 times 14" group work under the direction of Klaus Gallwitz in the Kunsthalle Baden-Baden.

In January 1972, Zangemeister became a clinical research associate at the Neurological University Clinic Hamburg-Eppendorf. Winning a scholarship from the German Research Association he worked with Lawrence W. Stark from 1978 to 1980 as Post-Doc at the University of California, Berkeley, at the Department of Physiological Optics, School of Optometry and Department of Biomedical Engineering, as well as at the University of California, San Francisco, at the Department of Neurosurgery and Neuro-Ophthalmology, with William F. Hoyt. Between 1981 and 2004, Zangemeister continued his cooperation with the Lawrence Stark laboratory as a visiting professor at the University of California,

Berkeley, and did research with the focus on visual-vestibular interaction in humans, model simulations of motor systems, especially head and eye movement, and scan path eye and gaze movements.

In 1982, he published his habilitation "Active head rotations and gaze coordination". In 1987, he was appointed full professor at the University of Hamburg. From 2000 until to his retirement in 2011, he was Head of the Neurological Outpatient Clinic at University Hospital Hamburg-Eppendorf. In his research lab, he still continues to supervise PhD students for joint research projects with PD Dr. Buhmann, funded by the Rickertsen Foundation Hamburg.

The aim of his work is to elucidate the neural processes of higher cognitive performance, such as visual perception, pictorial imagination, and other mental performances. Zangemeister is well-known internationally for his research and reflections on the clinical neurophysiological basis of attention and identification processes of image recognition and image assessment. His research focuses on the visual system, visual perception by the brain, as well as the neurobiological foundations of art and aesthetics. Especially the question of how neuroaesthetics can contribute to a better understanding in this context: Particularly the contribution of the scan path theory for active top down vision under normal and pathological conditions, i.e., real and virtual reality visual disturbances.

A long-term project of Zangemeister have been studies on the influence of motor deficits on gaze movements and attention. In correspondence, Zangemeister analyzed the connection between structural and synaesthetic content in the visual arts and selected classical modern literature. Zangemeister showed how the co-operation of synaesthetic qualia with hidden and multiple meanings has always been of great importance for the inner quality of pictorial works, as synaesthesia arises through a synchronous linking of a sense modality with one or more other sensory modalities. In art, synaesthesia refers to transfer and integration of sensory qualities and meanings within perceptual modalities in the visual arts, music and literature. The latter was an occasion for structural analysis in selected writings about Gottfried Benn and Robert Musil.

***Claudio M. Privitera*'s** research interests cover several aspects of biological and computational perception from a motor theory standpoint. In vision, he worked on Scanpath eye movements and visual attention, more recently, applying these domains to neuroaesthetics. His research interests are also in the area of the human pupillary mechanism with a specific emphasis on clinical, psychological and cognitive applications. He received the Laurea degree in Computer Science from the University of Pisa, Italy.From 1992 to 1995 he held a PhD fellowship within the National Research Program on Bioengineering working at DIST, Department of Informatics, Systems, and Telecommunications at the University of Genoa, Italy. In 1994, he worked at Laboratorie Scribens, École Polytechnique, Université de Montréal. From 1995 to 1997 he held a postdoctoral position at the University of California at Berkeley. He joined the Neurology and Telerobotics Units directed by Lawrence Stark in 1997 and until 2004. He taught for several years in the Mechanical Engineering Department. Currently he is still at the University of California at Berkeley working in the School of Optometry. In parallel with his basic scientific and academic interests he also has industry experience directing the R&D efforts of a few Silicon Valley companies. Presently, he holds the position of Chief Scientist at Neuroptics Inc.

single neuron recordings. Nor must we rely on indirect psychophysics studies that ask people to solve puzzles, and to measure their errors and reaction times.

With technologies such as non-invasive functional magnetic resonance imaging (fMRI), real-time brain activity patterns can be studied. Furthermore, in understanding "vision and perception", the role of eye movements and active looking may clarify how the visual brain dynamically controls and seeks out information in the external world. With the advent of imaging technology, a synthesis of neuropsychological, neurological imaging and physiological findings with art production and reception seems imminent and achievable.

Figure 1. Vermeer's painting "The Allegory of Painting".

2. Top Down Versus Bottom Up

Down through the ages, people in and out of the art world have debated how the communication between artist and viewer occurs. The two basic theories are the so-called "Top Down" (TD), and the "Bottom Up" (BU) approach. While the second chapter will discuss these theories in detail, a brief introduction here may be helpful.

The BU approach has been the most widely accepted theory in the past. It claims that people's eyes (their "visual brains") can be attracted and guided in a way that the creator of a picture can prescribe – such that the viewer's eye follows predetermined paths. This could involve moving to things previously not attended to, like a car suddenly appearing in the peripheral visual field. Or, in a painting, it could involve using features such as contrasts, patterns, colors or specific forms making use of so-called pre-attentive visual functions to attract the curiosity and attention of the viewer. This BU approach is thus widely used in advertising and public relations; as to command and direct visual attention is an undeniable advantage when presenting and conveying visual information.

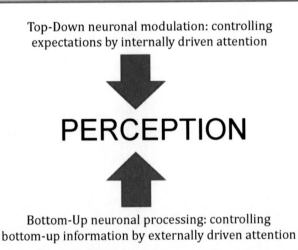

Figure 2. Top Down vs. Bottom Up.

In contrast to the BU approach is the top down (TD) approach. In the TD approach, the artists' internal model drives the creation of their art, e.g., a painting. Then, when a viewer looks at a particular painting, it activates many pre-existent models or images in their brain. Viewers try to match these models (or parts of them) with the picture in front of them. In the TD approach, both artist and viewer use their brain to generate a picture: one in the artists' brain and then on canvas, and one in the viewers' brain when looking at the painting. For the viewer, the picture must awaken a schema that approximates the painting. This schema must be stored in their modular brain in a somewhat similar way to the creative schema of the artist. In this way, viewers try to link with the picture's particular information – its message.

3. PERCEIVING AND INTERPRETING: THE VIEWER'S ROLE

As an historical example a figure from Buswell's book "How do people look at pictures?" [3] was selected.

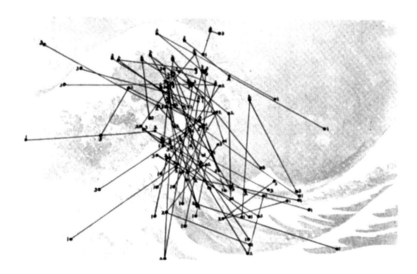

Figure 3. Eye movements viewing Hokusai's "Wave", from G. T. Buswell, 1935.

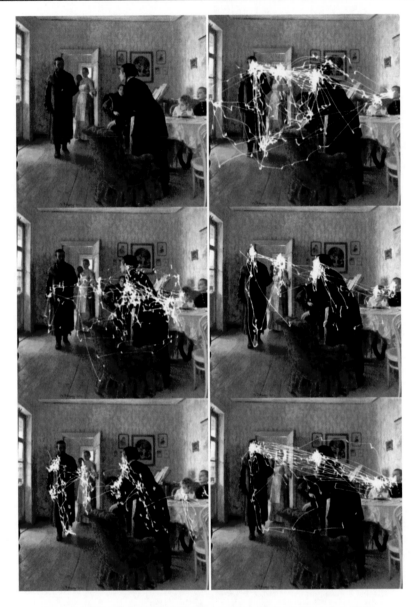

Figure 4. From Yarbus, 1967, "The unexpected visitor", by I. Repin, ca.1886.

Here the first three fixations of 50 subjects are shown freely viewing a picture by Hokusai "The Wave". It demonstrates overall similarity across many subjects focusing on the wave's form and direction – it is assumed that most viewers already have a preconceived understanding and internal model of what a wave is and what a wave looks like, and that this may well guide their successive eye movements when viewing the picture. The following example stems from Yarbus' book on "Eye Movements" from 1967 [4].

Here, a given task is the variable that influences the top down eye movements of one same subject in five different conditions (top-right: examine the painting freely, center-left: estimate the material circumstances of the family, center-right: assess the ages of the characters, bottom-left: remember the characters' clothes, bottom-right: surmise how long the "unexpected visitor" had been away). It demonstrates the high variability of the subject's EMs due to task-dependency underlying the TD function. An integral part of the TD approach is the concept of active looking. When we look at an object, our eyes "see" only 1-2 degrees of our fixation focus – the point we are specifically looking at – with a very high resolution, and in color, using the eye's "fovea". The periphery of our visual field has progressively lower resolution and is insensitive to color; however, it is very sensitive to dynamic, moving visual stimuli and contrasts. For example, compare the center with the peripheral part in Edgar Degas' "Beach Scene": It shows intuitively the large high resolution foveal part in the foreground, – whereas the low resolution picture parts are set to the periphery and the background.

Therefore we have to attend and follow a moving stimulus very closely to accurately perceive it with high resolution – like when we follow the flight path of an aeroplane. This of course, is a typical top down maneuver, since we decide in advance to fixate on and follow this object of interest to see it with optimal visual clarity. That is why eye movements, and the experiments involving them, play such a critical role in explaining and understanding the TD approach. When we view a painting, our eye focuses on curves, angles, line crossings, shadows and colours. In the BU scheme, (to exaggerate slightly), the viewer behaves more like a "reflex animal" that follows given environmental stimuli and cues: perhaps the drop of a line for example. In the TD scheme (also to exaggerate slightly), the viewer decides actively which pre-existent model could optimally match the picture she/he is looking at. In our example: a TD approach could consist of transgressing slightly upwards rather then following the drop of a line to try applying the model of a face to the picture; if the drop of the line is a nose, two circles above could be recognized as the eyes of a face.

Of course, while the matching process is going on between the viewer and the picture, there is a continuous exchange between TD and BU. In both cases we are looking at the painting or any object over some period of time. Thus we can focus on objects or regions of interest (ROIs) only in sequence: The duration of these fixations becomes an important parameter, since during longer lasting fixations of small areas – like when we view closely the face of a Rembrandt portrait – the initial model that the TD view applies, may be completed and complemented by some BU experiences of these ROIs. To "understand" a picture, these sequences of fixations while viewing a painting are indispensable. That there is a sequence of successive eye fixations while looking at pictures has been well proven – and it has led to the development of the "Scanpath Theory" by Noton and Stark, 1971 [5, 6]. This theory prescribes the sensory-motor sequence of these eye movements that carry fixations and visual perceptions of single regions of interest in the picture.

Figure 5. Foveal versus Peripheral vision – shown intuitively by the setting of E. Degas' 'Beach Scene', 1877.

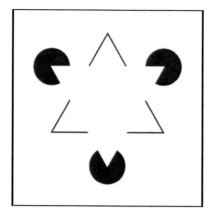

Figure 6. The Kaniza Triangle.

4. IT'S ALL AN ILLUSION:
VISUAL CONSTANCY, CLARITY, COMPLETENESS

Gestalt psychologists used a concept of "filling in" that they called the "Law of Praegnanz" to account for some filling in of shapes. The Kaniza triangle illusion is a good example: The corners defined leads to a notion of the whole.

Underlying the "Law of Praegnanz" was an analogy between brain processes and physical fields - like gravitational fields. Indeed, in their seminal work on Gestalt Psychology, Koffka, Kohler and Wertheimer [7, 8, 9] actually tried to measure electromagnetic fields in the brain spreading out and "filling in"; so their idea was more than a metaphor. In any case the psychophysical "organization" would be as "good" as possible. The psychological processes were driven supposedly by a number of processes. Uniformity, simplicity, closure of shapes are some of the descriptive names to these mental, perhaps physical processes at work. They approached a number of difficult problems like figure-ground separation (the segmentation of modern computer vision). How to get this? Their answer is, with internal and external forces producing the separation. The figure is made something thing-like, with an enclosed and as simple as possible shape; the ground is made stuff-like, driven by tendencies toward uniformity.

Another area where their speculations intersect with our own is in the area of eye movements and fixations. The refixation saccade was not an "reflex- arc" but rather was driven by the "praegnanz principle" of good organization which in this case is to place the figure in the center of the organized field. In some ways their's was a bottom-up theory in that a momentarily outstanding figure needs to be brought into the center. On the other hand they described eye movements as often "roaming". Their program was to describe behavior and they preceeded Gibson [10] in deciding that the geographical environment in a way governed perception since the behavior driven by these percepts had to be successful in the environment; perhpas they were more sophisticated than Gibson, who chose to ignore any internal processes and just deal with the remarkable fact that behavior driven by percepts was indeed in accordance with the environment or distant stimulus. They asked "why do things look as they do?" and their answer rested on internal processes of organization of perceptions that itself produced patterns that led to sucessful behaviors by an ego with memory and capable of learning by association, but also with innate processes of organization working away.

5. ART, NEUROSCIENCE AND THE SENSE OF BEAEUTY

An artist is not necessarily more sensitive than an art-lover, and is often less so than a teenager; but his sensitivity is of a different order. To be romantic is not to be a novelist, to indulge in daydreams is not to be a poet. Just as a musician loves music and not nightingales, and a poet, poems and not sunsets, a painter is not primarily a man who is thrilled by figures and landscapes. He is essentially one who loves pictures. "Those to whom art as such means nothing see it as a means of recording life's poignant moments, or of conjuring them up in the imagination. Thus they tend to confuse story-telling with the novel, representation with painting. Most men would have no more ideas about painting, sculpture and literature than they have about architecture - which to their eyes, as painting often does, seems merely decoration on the grand scale – were it not that sometimes they have fleeting intimations of that "something behind everything" on which all religions are founded; when gazing, for example, into the vastness of the night, or when they are confronted by a birth, a death, or even a certain face. Ignorance may partly explain the masses' dislike for modern art, but here is also a vague distaste for something in it which they feel to be a betrayal" (A. Malraux, 1964 [11]).

a. Why Understanding the Cake Doesn't Make It Taste Less Good

We are aware, in fact we have been warned, that professional art historians and critics, in most instances, do not want the world of empirical neuro-psychology and information science infused into the world of art, its history and its complexities, be they social, artistic, historical, or media dependent. They believe these sciences to be superficial, and of lesser help in "understanding" art. C. P. Snow in his famous Rede lecture on "The Two Cultures" [12] pointed out some basic differences between scientists and literary intellectuals:

Figure 7a. Bellini: "Giovane donna davanti allo specchio", ca.1515.

Figure 7b. Caravaggio: "Judith Beheading Holofernes", ca. 1598.

"The non-scientists have a rooted impression that the scientists are shallowly optimistic, unaware of man's condition. On the other hand, the scientists believe that the literary intellectuals are totally lacking in foresight, peculiarly unconcerned with their brother men, in a deep sense anti-intellectual, anxious to restrict both art and thought to existential moment."

It may appear that in the last forty years some of this controversy has vanished, and rightfully so. Besides the two cultures there has grown a third culture linking both neuroscience and the humanities. The many trials to relate modern, particularly conceptual art with scientific processes, as well as the link between philosophy and neuroscience in more recent times by neuroscientists and philosophers demonstrates this. On the other hand, there are still similar reservations by literary intellectuals as noted in the citation by C. P. Snow against the mixture and "shallow" interpretation of artistic work by applying scientific methods. Readers who would believe this is solely a book that reviews eye movement experiments on paintings would be wrong. This book explains the link between the active visual mind and its use of eye movements while viewing artistic pictures. For example, some people might feel there is an inherent, philosophic problem in ascertaining a successful explanation of eye movement behavior using data attained through viewing paintings as diverse and different as, e.g., by Bellini, Caravaggio or Monet (Figures 7-8). These experiments, they would say, tell us nothing about the painting's content, or background, or its possible appreciation.

Figure 8. View of the river Thames by Monet: "Fog on the Thames" 1903.

Others would go further. Assume that experiments such as recording, analyzing, and interpreting scanpath eye movements under specific stimulus conditions could explain the viewer's response to a painting by, e.g., Caravaggio or Monet. Furthermore, assume that these responses could be effectively recognized and distinguished from the responses to other similar works, or to the responses of other people to that same Caravaggio or Monet. Even then these explanations would be divorced from the viewers' interest in the picture as art. Critics would say: 'The spectator loves Caravaggio for many reasons, and none of them have to do with eye movements.'

In art, if someone claims that our interest in Caravaggio can be traced to eye movement recordings, then that person has, of course, not explained Caravaggio, but something having to do with eye movements. Whether this something is important or irrelevant clearly depends on the question we ask. If we ask the very general but important question "what is the meaning of this picture?" the eye movement recordings appear rather irrelevant. But if we ask the question "how is our brain using our eyes to perceive and eventually "understand" the artist's message resulting in the viewed picture?", the eye movement recordings become highly interesting. Interesting, because they can tell us a lot about the workings of the active looking brain, as it matches its models to the picture, to communicate through the picture with the artist.

These objections involve a typical, sometimes willful, misunderstanding of the links between art and science. If we apply the scanpath theory, together with current neuroimaging and empirical neuropsychological knowledge to artistic pictures, it does not necessarily mean that we are trying to explain Caravaggio or Monet, their paintings, and why one loves them! The scanpath theory will be discussed in greater detail later. But for now, consider it a way of explaining how the eye moves when looking at an object. Thus, it is obviously important in the active looking process of the TD approach, in that it examines the successive sensory-motor foveations following the initial internal model of the viewer resulting in a mental image of the viewed object – a process that may be repeated several times. By enumerating historical, sociological, or formal (i.e., formal contents of the picture) reasons, art historians might explain why we prefer one painting to another. But they will not be able to really prove this; even with the application of formalistic "art theories". Nor will historians be able to accurately describe the fine instruments and tools we possess as human beings – tools and instruments used in viewing and perceiving artistic pictures. These are the tools that artists, throughout human history, have used and experimented with – rather like scientists, certainly not like art historians.

What we talk about in this book is not the quality of socio-historical, opinions and feelings about art. Rather, we show the reader how the "active looking brain" generally guides our eyes when we view art. We show how this delicate tool works, how visual perception and visual cognition work closely together, while we move our eyes.

Links between art and science exist and have existed for a long time. An early example was Leonardo's research on optics, perspective and colour vision. David Hockney has remarked [13] that in the 16th and 17th century many artists tried to "copy nature" through the use of optical instruments like magnifying lenses or other optical devices which had just been developed. Impressionist painting took up the research results of its time on physiological optics. More recently, artists have used techniques developed in applied science such as CT-scan radiographs of the brain for artistic pictorial messages, whereas others have exploited the digital world of moving pictures (mostly videos) with varying success.

The pitfalls of pure bottom up explanations for how we look at art are obvious. Without an idea (model, preconception) concerning the many implications of a painting – be them religious, semantic, historical, sociological, political or technical – the viewer will never be able to detect or appreciate the "message" of the painting with clarity. However, in many instances this viewer would still be able to match pictorial content with general 'common' knowledge of the world; perhaps natural or historical settings or facial expressions for example. Again, this would not mean a viewing from bottom up. Rather it would be a more simplistic, less sophisticated application of top down viewing of that painting. A complete bottom up viewing of figurative artistic pictures is hardly conceivable: The non-sophisticated, naive observer of art would still use some preconceived models of how pictures should and in fact could look like, such as "realistic and naturalistic" views of the environment. The viewer would be lost, as in fact many are, with abstract, i.e., not only "abstracted", conceived paintings by Malevich, Rothko or Pollock – even though he might appreciate shapes and colors of these paintings. Despite this, the naive viewer would probably still look for some known (top down model) shapes etcetera.

Therefore the question arises: What is so specific about the top down versus bottom up information seeking process when viewing art? What distinguishes it from everyday picture perception?

Understanding the processes of vision, cognition, perception within the background of the "new neurology" and information theory puts together and systemizes many facts known from neurology and psychology that can help the viewers, be they specialists or naive. It enables them to be more aware and apply consciously their personal, subjective models of works of art. Knowing and using the top down approach in this case will give them a more refined way to view, recognize and finally perceive different works of art as messages of artistic models, also including some fuzziness in their "signal to noise level", "what", i.e., the formal and emotional information, the artist really had in mind to communicate to the viewer. The viewer will be more conscious of his own limited way of viewing artwork. With his more conscious explication of the workings of top down and bottom up mechanisms in this recognition process, he will be able to better follow the intentions of a given painting, i.e., the aspects of the model that the artist used when he created the painting.

b. What about the Sense of Beauty in Works of Art, When We Use Our Top Down Model of Viewing?

The quest for beauty has been of major concern in artists and viewers of art. In fact, the discussion of the "beauty" of a particular painting is often quite controversial; frequently it has been used to disqualify new, later on so called avangardistic art – as an example see the specific "style" of the Italian painter Caravaggio in late 16th century. Another example is the advent of impressionism in the 19th century seen in two pictures by Monet. In both instances the new style, i.e., the new model of the specific perception of the environment that artists would apply and show in their paintings, would be more enthusiastically welcomed and appreciated by insiders (young fellow artists, some art collectors) and dismissed by most of the rest that was still used to and applied somewhat more old-fashioned models: they would say that Caravaggio's style was "awkwardly realistic, brutal"; or simply "wrong" compared to nature – as with the impressionists. This example sends us a second message. Art, artistic pictures and the overall information content they transmit, is subject to dynamic change over the course of time. There are individual changes with respect to the viewer – such as state of mind, emotion, knowledge of art, and context when viewing the painting. But there are also more "global" changes, i.e., changes related to socio-historical facts such as differences and fluctuations with respect to culture, common appreciation or historical political changes as, e.g., in post-revolution Russia.

People believe that "sense of beauty" may be universal. This may well be true with respect to universal "primitives" such as symmetry, geometrical shapes, or general facial perception – as we now know from neuroimaging studies. However, this kind of "sense of beauty" is heavily influenced by our preconceptions, expectations, and therefore also by cultural and historical differences of artist and viewer. The point is that our view of information exchange between artist and viewer – with the picture as the message – is embedded in the more general, informational content of subjective, local, regional, nowadays sometimes global context of perceptions preoccupations expectations about art.

Is the Contemplation of Beauty Confusing the Depiction of Ideas?

Plato (Symposion 211d): If there is anything worthwhile to live for it is the contemplation of beauty. Thus every sort of confusion is revealed within us; and this is that weakness of the human mind on which the art of conjuring and of deceiving by light and shadow and other ingenious devices imposes, having an effect upon us like magic. But in all this variety of circumstances is man at unity with himself or rather, as in the instance of sight there was confusion and opposition in his opinions about the same things, so here also is there not strife and inconsistency in his life. The conclusion at which he was seeking to arrive was that painting or drawing, and imitation in general, when doing their own proper work, are far removed from truth.

Later, *Aristotle* showed three modes of production, one by nature, from within, distinguished from techne, production from without; then, within techne, between production by design or according to an end, and Poiesis, bringing into being from nonbeing. *Aristotle's view* seems to be much more realistic and could be applied even to modern art: mimesis as the artist's model showing up; also "a kind of thing that might happen" which reminds us almost of concept art and fluxus. Two main differences to Plato are obvious in Aristotle's thinking: The value of imitation and the benefits of the kinds of emotional gratifications we receive from poetry. Whether the answer he gives is satisfactory for all art is an important question, especially considering nonrepresentational art of the twentieth century. In defense of mimesis Aristotle expresses art's concern with reality, "to describe, not the thing that has happened, but a kind of thing that might happen." The medieval church and philosophers as Scotus Enigena held that true beauty belonged to God. The basic material of arts was believed as the relics and depositories of paganism.

Descartes stands for the close relation between science and art, particularly visual art, in that he made great progress in explaining and connecting the knowledge of his time about physiology of vision and perception with his philosophy of knowledge applied to art. In his knowledge about physiology of vision and perception Descartes is the most advanced modern thinker about art before the arrival of the 19th century scientific revolution. His understanding of an ego-centrically shaped perception exchanging its specific views including eye movements with the world fits well into our suggestion of prevailing Top down mechanisms in art.

Hume's theory of art is consistent with his general position. Taste is the primary notion, for there is no authority beyond taste for the evaluation of works of art. A standard of taste, however, can be derived from the workings of the mind. To many philosophers, this kind of analysis is psychologistic, and offers no foundation for a theory of art. We may say, then, that Hume poses the central problem of the philosophy of art, whether any theory can do more than describe the workings of the human mind when confronted with works of beauty and power. So Hume, in his view of taste as the primary notion with respect to art, is not in line with the exchange of Top down models between artist and viewer through artwork. His "taste" appears to be a Bottom up creation standardized for everyone. Hume is most famous for taken up empiricism. He is best known for his powerful and effective arguments that all our knowledge comes from experience but that experience offers no unassailable foundation for knowledge. He argues that causation can only be understood as constant conjunction, the linking of events in the mind based on its past experience. Similarly, he argues that morality is founded on internal principles of sympathy and sentiments toward others. The constant theme of Hume's position is a reliance on mechanisms internal to the mind and a skepticism toward the foundations underlying experience. *Kant,* in his first Critique defines understanding under causal necessity, and the second Critique defines reason under the concept of freedom. Into this general system, Kant brings fundamental questions concerning the nature of art. He denies that art falls under the concepts of necessity or freedom. He also denies that art is a form of understanding or morality. With this, he offers a powerful argument for the uniqueness and autonomy of art by denying that aesthetic judgement and taste are objective. Nevertheless, although subjective, judgements of beauty must be universal, shareable by everyone who possesses good taste. In relation to beauty, Kant offers a community of taste ungoverned by concepts. Kant also offers a theory of the sublime, where the infinite, beyond concepts, appears in art, and of genius, the capacity to produce apart from rules. Kant's theory of taste has had a great influence, supporting a view of art for art's sake, independent of the human or natural world. His view of genius was deeply influential in Romanticism. Kant is "modern" in his reasoning about the nature of art: excluding the meaning of artworks and the concepts of necessity, freedom, understanding and morality concerning the nature of art.

Some differences between the approaches of information theorists involved in memory research and neuropsychological aestheticians have been noted by Berlyne and others [14]. Information theorists emphasize the practical or instrumental value of perception. Hence, they maintain that the "transient products" of preliminary physical or sensory analyses may be discarded in favor of the results of "deeper" semantic analyses. They also argue that a person is only consciously aware of the level of analysis that receives attention and extensive processing. From the perspective of neuropsychological aesthetics, all levels of processing, including sensory and semantic analyses, are of equal importance. Furthermore, the aesthetic set of the spectator sensitizes him to all levels of analysis. These "levels" may be processed simultaneously or in parallel. This implies that the aesthetic set involves a broader mode of attention, which can grasp interactions among the levels. In light of these criticisms the following example is very instructive; two individuals are about to enter an art gallery that is hosting an exhibition of Cubist paintings. One of these spectators knows very little about art and has never experienced the work of Picasso and his contemporaries in any intensive way. The other person is a devoted admirer of this school of painting, and is well informed concerning its fundamental attributes and subject matter.

The information theorists and neuropsychologists who favour the behaviouristic perspective would have us believe that both these individuals would pass through the same three stages of perception, and in the same sequence. Perhaps they would allow for the fact that the expert spectator might traverse them more quickly. Yet, it seems unlikely that speed of processing is the only difference. The expert possesses an aesthetic set which is already highly tuned to the sensory and physical qualities of Cubism. Moreover, he may also already possess many memories and attendant emotions derived from past exposure. Thus, is there any reason to believe that he needs to go through stages at all? On the other hand, his interest in Cubism may be based solely on an appreciation of its physical and sensory qualities. He does not need to proceed to any other stages, since this is the effective locus of what Cubism means to him. In this case, the first stage could in effect represent a consolidation of attributes from the various "stages". The viewer may never have negotiated his way through them sequentially.

In contrast, we may consider the novice spectator. Perhaps his aesthetic set constrains him to search only for semantic content, and for the "realistic" qualities of painting. He does not enter the first stage, which is sensory and physical, other than in the sense that he must register the paintings in his visual system. The syntactic qualities are bypassed in his search for quality of realistic representation. In addition, the works evoke no memories or associations, since he simply considers the paintings in the same way one would view a postcard. When stages become interchangeable, when one stage is not a consolidation of its predecessor, or when a given stage may be unnecessary owing to aesthetic set, we are left with a series of processes which cannot be understood as "stages" in any accepted sense. Of foremost importance are the principle of aesthetic set, and the plasticity of perception itself. Depending on his skills, the spectator may analyze and act on perceptions in various ways. The modes of viewing which he adopts may be subject to spontaneous revision. The situational context that the viewer finds himself in, and his frame of mind, are crucial contributors to the fluidity of his perception.

6. A BOOK FOR THE ART WORLD AND THE WORLD OF SCIENCE

By using a positive background – the results of eye movement studies, cognitive neuroscience, information science and neuroimaging – we present a model to explain the links between the worlds of art and science. It tries to answer the question: How can we better understand visual art by using our neurological scientific knowledge? And thus it is for those who want to understand the real world implications of scientific advances concerning the process of visual communication.

In other words, we endeavor to demonstrate a link between art and neurological sciences, and what each field can learn from the other: To demonstrate how the TOP-DOWN approach pervades most art, rather than the formerly so popular BOTTOM-UP approach – we show the implications of the TD approach in how we perceive and interpret art. Since we want non-scientists to read and appreciate the book, we have tried to keep the language and the notes on special results of neuroscience easy and understandable with limited scientific terminology. The only advised prerequisites to reading and enjoying this book are an interest in art and the brain.

REFERENCES

[1]   C. Shannon and W. Weaver, *A mathematical theory of communication*. Urbana Illinois: University of Illinois Press., 1949.

[2]   O. Sacks, "Travels through a mindscape," *The Economist*, no. September 5, pp. 1–2, 2015.

[3]   G. T. Buswell, *How people look at pictures*, 1st ed. Chicago: University of Chicago Press, 1935.

[4]   A. Yarbus, *Eye Movements*. Plenum NewYork, 1967.

[5]   D. Noton and L. W. Stark, "Scanpaths in eye movements during pattern perception," *Science*, vol. 171, pp. 308–311, 1971.

[6]   D. Noton and L. W. Stark, "Eye movements and visual perception," *Sci. Am.*, vol. 244, pp. 34–53, 1972.

[7]   K. Koffka, *Principles of Gestalt psychology*. New York: Harcourt, Brace, & World, 1935.

[8]   W. Köhler, *Gestaltpsychologie*. H Liverlight New York, 1981.

[9]   M. Wertheimer, "Gestalt theory, The general theoretical situation, Laws of organization in perceptual forms," in *A source book of Gestalt psychology*, W. D. Ellis, Ed. London, England: Routledge & Kegan Paul, 1938, pp. 1-16-94.

[10] J. J. Gibson, *The perception of the visual world*. The Riverside Press, Cambridge, Massachusetts, 1950.

[11] A. Malraux, *The Voices of Silence: Man and his Art*. Princeton: Princeton Univ. Press, 1978.

[12] C. Snow, *The Two Cultures (1959)*. Cambridge,UK: Cambridge University Press, 1993.

[13] Lawrence Weschler, "The Looking Glass: The Modern Master David Hockney has a Theory", *New Yorker*, no. January 31, pp. 65–75, 2000.

[14] D. E. Berlyne, *Aesthetics and psychobiology*. New York: Appleton-Century- Crofts, 1971.

Chapter 2

THE NEUROLOGY OF LOOKING:
BOTTOM UP/TOP DOWN VISION

Low-Level and High-Level vision are interwoven. Biological vision begins with measurements of the amount of light reflected from surfaces in the environment on to the eye, generating the retinal image. A main goal of low-level visual processes is to recover properties of the surrounding environment. Vision proceeds in stages, with each stage producing increasingly more useful descriptions of the world. The process of vision can be viewed as the construction of a series of representations of visual information with explicit computation that transforms one representation into the next. Later representations for vision capture information necessary to solve complex tasks. The main difference between low and high-level visual processes is in the kind of knowledge they use: On the way to individual identification an object is often classified first more broadly as a face or a car. Following the initial classification some stored models will become more likely than others. Knowledge and expectation about the current situation can thereby be used to influence the activation or priming of a subset of models that will then become preferential sources for descending sequences. Context can have powerful influence on the processing of visual information.

Recognition in the sequence-seeking scheme can become faster and more efficient by the learning of past successful sequences. Following practice, out of the huge number of possible sequences those that proved useful in the past will be explored with higher priority in future uses of the viewer.

Kant's take on eye movement theory relates to his Critique of pure Reason where he speaks about knowledge as a principal problem of philosophy: A thinking that goes back to the pre-Socratic philosophers and Plato – and a parallel to the brain as a knowledge seeking neural machinery.

From the large number of external stimuli that we perceive and that are transmitted by afferent nerve fiber tracts to our brain, we consciously perceive only few by sorting out those stimuli that are meaningful to us in a given situation. Especially in the somatosensory system it is well established that gating mechanisms on the spinal, thalamic, and cortical level mediate this selection of information. This gating is also true for the visual system.

1. EYE MOVEMENTS (EM)

a. Low-Level and High-Level Vision

The various types and control of EM contribute differently to vision and are characterized by specific dynamics: Saccades (Figure 9a and their Main Sequence, Figure 9b) are very fast voluntary EM of up to 900°/sec velocity and an amplitude working range of 1° to 25°. Microsaccades involuntary EM, are smaller, below 1°, and slower, and they are generated within a fixation. Other slower EM are: pursuit EM of up to 30°/sec for fixation of moving targets and nystagmic EM, that are combined of a fast saccadic-like and a slow pursuit-like phase (e.g., vestibular and optokinetic nystagmus); this is also the case when we move our head in pursuing some object of interest: we "exchange" head position for eye position, i.e., the eye catches first the target and then the head moves toward the same direction to the target, while the vestibular ocular reflex (VOR) brings the eye back to the primary position.

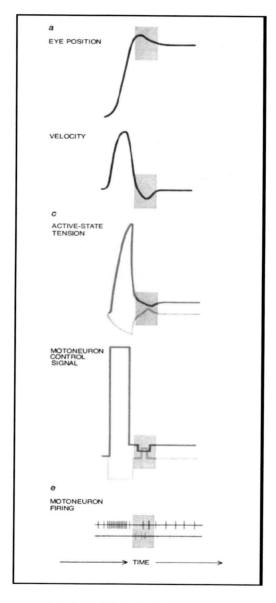

Figure 9a. From top – as functions of time (abscissa, 50 ms) – eye position, velocity, active state tension, abstracted motoneural control signal, firing pattern of neural control signal.

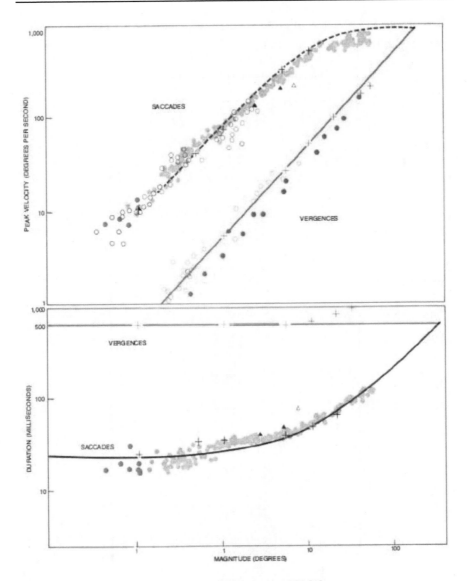

Figure 9b. Main Sequence of EM by Bahill & Stark 1979 [1].

Two further functions are important for fixations, especially when sequential: The resolution of the retina with its high resolution fovea of about 1° in the center, and its low resolution periphery that is especially sensitive to movement. The second important aspect that permits us to concatenate successive fixations to one stable continuous visual impression of the world is the so-called *saccadic suppression:* between saccadic EM there is a highly decreased visual resolution, that suppresses any smearing of the intervening pictures while the eyes are moving.

Most important for stability of fixation during movements of the head and/or body, and also of the fixated target, are the pursuit EM, the OKN – optokinetic nystagmus and the VOR – vestibular ocular reflex, that takes the eyeball back to the center field of vision when the head moves.

Biological vision begins with measurements of the amount of light reflected from surfaces in the environment on to the eye. The retinal image provided by the photoreceptors can be thought of as a large array of continuously changing numbers that represent light intensities. From this array of light measurements the visual system does not achieve an understanding of what is in the scene in a single step.

The blur and deflection of stripes of a viewed diagonal black and white pattern with horizontal EM of higher velocity from left to right – i.e., larger amplitudes according to the Main Sequence – has been shown for saccades of different amplitudes by Perez and Peli ([2] Figure 10). They could demonstrate that without cortical, saccadic suppression our visual world very often would be "smeared".

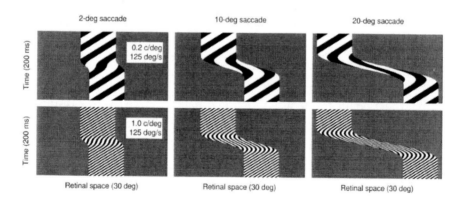

Figure 10. Shows the blur and deflection of stripes of a viewed diagonal black and white pattern with horizontal EM of higher velocity from left to right – i.e., larger amplitudes according to the Main Sequence (after: MA Perez and E Peli [2] with permission).

Vision proceeds in stages, with each stage producing increasingly more useful descriptions of the world. The process of vision can be viewed as the construction of a series of representations of visual information with explicit computation that transforms one representation into the next.

b. Stages of Vision - Top Down Versus Bottom Up

Representations proposed for the early stages of vision first capture information that can be extracted simply and directly from the initial image, such as the location and description of significant intensity changes or edges in the image. Subsequent representations capture the local geometry or 3-D-shape of visible surfaces in the scene, represented as the orientation or depth of surfaces at each location in the scene. Many familiar visual processes, such as the analysis of movement, binocular stereopsis, surface shading, texture, and color, contribute to the computation of these early visual representations. We refer to these early stages of vision as low-level vision. A main goal of low-level visual processes is to recover properties of the surrounding environment. The representations that they deliver can be evaluated on the basis of their validity, that is, whether the results they deliver are correct and accurate.

Later representations for vision capture information necessary to solve complex tasks such a navigation through the environment, manipulation of objects, and recognition. The visual processes involved in accomplishing these tasks are often referred to as high-level vision. Although there is no well-defined boundary between low- and high-level vision, the distinction is useful. The main difference between low and high-level visual processes is in the kind of knowledge they use. Low-level vision relies on assumptions regarding the general physical properties of objects, such as continuity and rigidity. High-level tasks, such as recognition, knowledge that we have acquired about specific objects, such as their shape and perhaps the transformations that they may undergo.

Studies of visual recognition have shown the need and the feasibility of using top down processing as an integral part of the recognition process.

The use of top down processing in viewing includes the use of stored information required to deal with the effects of viewing direction, illumination, occlusion, and object deformation. Consequently, the top downtop down processing is expected to be more extensive then the bottom up part (Figure 2).

The general view expressed by Hubel and Wiesel in describing their findings regarding the visual cortex [3, 4] emphasizes the bottom up direction. This informal model regards visual information processing as the successive extraction of increasingly elaborate images features. Different cell types in the visual cortex, in particular simple, complex, and hyper-complex V1 units, were originally thought to form the first stages of this hierarchy.

In contrast with this approach, more recent studies argue in favour of a balanced combination of bottom up and top down processing. Recognition, including the difficult tasks of compensating for the effects of viewing direction, illumination, occlusion and object deformation, can benefit from the use of information associated with objects and object classes, acquired through past experience or as promoting.

Information processing in the visual cortex is therefore the capacity to combine efficiently bottom up processing starting at the image and proceeding to high-level cortical areas, with top down processing, starting at stored object representations, and proceeding from high to low visual areas.

The structure of the cortex clearly supports this possibility: A major characteristic of cortical interconnections is the reciprocity of the connections between visual areas. If a visual area in the cortex sends ascending connections to another visual area higher up in the hierarchy of visual processing, then, as a general rule, the second area sends reciprocal connections to the first.

Bottom-up signals have been scientifically studied for many years. First, the eye has to receive photons that excite the retina at the back of the eye and so send signals of what is "out there" to the brain for re-cognition. This has been described by theories of noise in photon packets and in cellular processes. The retinal periphery mostly with rods and only some cones can acquire a low resolution image of the current scene, but is very sensitive to movement of and within the visual surround. The fovea with its high resolution and color capabilities acquires the essential high resolution picture that we "see" or are aware of most of the time.

Bottom-Up: Aristotle, philosophy of art and aesthetics

As early as in the times of the pre-Socratic philosophers the bottom up view of [visual] perception was an important point of discussion [5]. Parmenides wrote on perception "Utterances" (his description):

"Do not let much-experienced have force you along this road, to let use an aimless eye and an echoing ear and a tongue, but judge by argument the much contending refutation uttered by me."

These lines do not argue for skepticism. But many scholars find in them a general rejection of sense-perception, although the lines say both more and less than that. First, the lines mention the tongue; and the tongue is the organ of speech as well as of taste. So, Parmenides has in mind not gustatory illusions but rather the perils inherent in ordinary language. Parmenides was an enemy of the senses and he "hurled the senses out of truth" (pseudo-Plutarch, A 22). But that enmity is left implicit in Parmenides' poem: There is no formed argument for skepticism in the text, and no explicit statement of skepticism.

Other than his teacher Plato, who did not believe in the "reality" of the visual world, Aristotle was interested in bottom up processes: The value of imitation and the benefits of the kinds of emotional gratifications we receive from poetry. Whether the answer he gives is satisfactory for all art is an important question, especially considering nonrepresentational art of the twentieth century. Aristotle's writings –The Poetics – are the important defense of mimesis. Not as Plato describes painting in Book X of the Republic, painting is an imitation of particular things, but a concern with reality, "to describe, not the thing that has happened, but a kind of thing that might happen."

Concerning the peripheral, bottom up-ness of deceptive paintings the historical writer Plinius wrote:

"The contemporaries and rivals of Zeuxis were Timanthes, Androcydes, Eupompus, Parrhasius. This last, it is recorded, entered into a competition with Zeuxis. Zeuxis produced a picture of grapes so dexterously represented that birds began to fly down to eat from the painted vine. Whereupon Parrhasius designed so lifelike a picture of a curtain that Zeuxis, proud of the verdict of the birds, requested that the curtain should now be drawn back and the picture displayed. When he realized his mistake, with a modesty that did him honor, he yielded up the palm, saying that whereas he had managed to deceive only birds, Parrhasius had deceived an artist."

So we can see how the optimal visual deception – certainly something that played with the lower level vision of the viewer plus his expectations following the initial stimulus – was regarded as a perfect artistic demonstration.

Some sixteen hundred years later, G. Berkeley begins his Principles of human knowledge by insisting that all objects of knowledge are ideas, describing:

"the ideas actually imprinted on the senses in separate groups of colors, hard and soft, and insisting that a thing is simply a collection of these which have been observed to accompany each other."

A few paragraphs later, he explains that the main objections to it come from the belief in abstract ideas:

"Can there be a nicer strain of abstraction than to distinguish the existence of sensible objects from their being perceived, so as to conceive them existing unperceived?"

With respect to art, the assumption is evident, that the objects of perception are indivisible, isolated sensibilia lying behind his treatment of objectivity. He was very far from denying the distinction between objective and subjective, or between real and illusory ideas. As he says in the *Second Dialogue between Hylas and Philonous*:

"It is evident that the things I perceive are my own ideas, and that no idea can exist unless it be in a mind. Nor is it less plain that these ideas or things by me perceived, exist independently of my mind."

In general, the hypotheses of "top down" and "bottom-up" can be used with different, but interchangeable meanings. Anatomically, top down influences are equated with the activity of feedback connections in a processing hierarchy, i.e., a system of interconnected modules, in which "higher" centers are activated later and contain more abstract representations than "lower" areas. Whereas bottom-up denotes feedforward information flow. Psychologically, the two concepts refer to the distinction between hypothesis/expectation-driven processing on one hand, and stimulus-driven processing on the other. Here, the subject could be controlled largely by a sensory stimulus, or dominated by intrinsic factors such as attention, memory, or expectation of forthcoming sensory events. This is the case in many situations, where the properties of the "whole" determine the perception of the "parts".

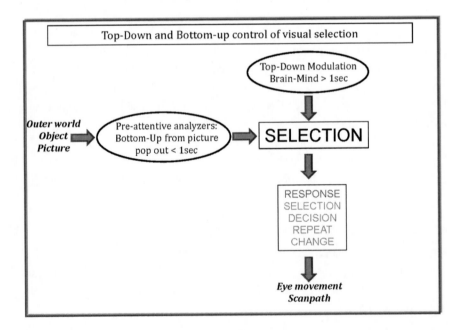

Figure 11. Top-down visual selection schema.

Often it could take longer to identify the parts than to respond behaviorally to features of the whole. This global-precedence effect, which provides one of many examples of the contextual modulation of perceptual items, can be considered as another variant of top down – the perceptual idea of top down. Finally, top down could be referred to as a dynamical state, in which large scale dynamics can have a predominant influence on local neuronal behavior by "enslaving" or "enhancing" local processing elements. Synchronized populations in a network might entrain other neurons after some time to become part of the same overall assembly, which is a spatially distributed set of cells that are activated in a coherent fashion and are part of the same representation. This results from the spread of synchronized activity through lateral connections. It could correspond to the incorporation of some contents into a broader context, leading to a reinterpretation of the represented item. This idea of top down does not require a processing hierarchy, but the dynamic 'capture' of neurons into a larger assembly could occur between areas at the same processing level or within one area. This "dynamicist" view assumes that the intrinsic processing dynamics of a cognitive system are a crucial variable for expressing goals or expectations. These correspond then to states of large-scale integration in the system.

The whole concept of top down is more than the idea of feedback signal flow. It encompasses a whole class of phenomena. The above notions of top down are interchangeable, as they partly apply at different levels of description (Figure 11).

Often it appears as if our eye movements are guided by catchy, visually interesting or seemingly important points of interest. Our eye may jump directly to this spot of a picture and we may believe it is because of the special design, which reflects the arrangement of contrasts, borderlines, colors, depth and special subfeatures especially with respect to the primary region of interest (ROI). This type of viewing strategy would resemble a bottom up approach of viewing, where no cognitive model of the picture, i.e., perceptual hypothesis which has to be tested against sensory experience, is present and the eyes' movements and fixations appear to be highly influenced by the features of the image. Multi-item boundary and surface groupings influence visual search. They may not represent the perceptual components upon which the search process is based. But the identification of a grouping that includes multiple items speeds the search process by reducing the total number of candidate visual regions that have to be investigated serially. Factors which influence boundary and surface grouping, such as featural contrast, item spacing, and spatial arrangement alter the number of visual regions to be explored, yielding variations in search time.

If in some instances bottom up mechanisms drive the formation of these emergent perceptual units, then limits must exist on the capacity of semantic or even visual definitions of target items to exert top down influence over preattentive grouping mechanisms. The ability of bottom up processing to distinguish ecological objects accurately depends on a certain amount of autonomy or resistance to top down interference. Otherwise, it would routinely result in perceptual illusions. Of course, perceptual grouping indeed will often be guided by top down processes. However, some groupings may "emerge" from the structure of the scene input without the help of top down influences. Early studies on eye movements while subjects viewed scenes and pictures showed that visual exploration or search is not random, but that eve movements are related to the content of the scene ([6, 7, 8, 9, 10] and especially Yarbus 1967 [11]). The pattern of eye movements, mainly consisting of fixations and saccades, could be altered by the pictures that were observed and by the instructed task. Noton and Stark ([12, 13]) experimentally measured sequences of eye movements while pictures were viewed and suggested that the repetitive sequences of saccadic eye movements, the Scanpath, represented a playing out of an internal control sequence from a sensory-motor representation of a picture or scene in the brain.

A strength of bottom up is the rapid response to environmental stimuli. If the field of view is unchanged, i.e., no change in the area and no eye and head movement - then everything which is relevant is processed within the first second [14]. Bottom up starting later than 1 second has then a minor role. On the other hand, top down needs very often initially a recognition performance; because only after an object is detected in the visual field, top down can take place in response thereto. In this respect, the top down effect takes place usually late, i.e., after a 1 second. Even though capture itself within the attended window is completely stimulus driven i.e., bottom up, the extent to which subjects divide their attention across the display – the size of the window – is under top down control. Salience computations are restricted to the attentional window of the observer. When observers are in a focused mode, selection of the next item is random [15]. While the size of the attentional window is under top down control, *within the attentional window* top down control cannot preclude attention from being captured by the most salient feature [16, 17]. Only by adjusting the size of the attentional window, the initial sweep of information through the brain may be altered in a top–down way. A very early top down influence happens, when a window of attention is triggered *before the appearance* of a stimulus. This is the case with anticipation/prediction of a target of interest: Then, the top down influence is already there before bottom up activity has even started.

c. Initial Identification and Classification

On the way to individual identification an object is often classified first more broadly as a face, a car, a bird, and the like. The classification may even be non-unique, that is a number of competing interpretations may still exist at this stage. Following the initial classification some stored models will become more likely than others, and will be activated and processed with higher priority. For example, an object may be classified as a face prior to its individual identification, and following classification, face-related sequences will be expanded preferentially. Biologically, fast classification will involve the activation (or inhibition) of – sometimes preset – high-level patterns on the descending stream together with the lower-level ascending patterns, resulting in the preferred activation of the selected patterns. The fast initial selection of subsets of models will not be limited to the activation of object models at a single "topmost" level; intermediate models at different levels along the descending stream can also be activated and serve as the starting points for descending sub-sequences. For example, in addition to the selection of a complete face model, intermediate models of face-parts can also be activated, and perhaps also be stored models of some basic image configurations.

d. Expectation and Context

A second mechanism for a top down model selection is provided by the effects of expectation and context. Temporal and spatial correlations can influence the likelihood of different models. Knowledge about the current situation can thereby be used to influence the activation or priming of a subset of models that will then become preferential sources for descending sequences.

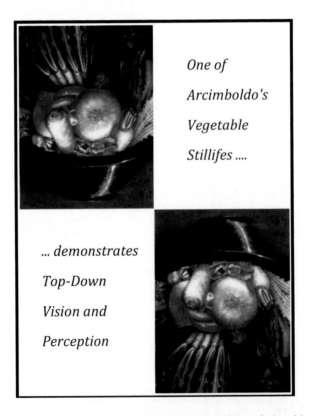

Figure 12. The vegetable head by Arcimboldo: example of the relationship between bottom-up and top down. a. bowl; 180 deg turned: b. head.

Context can have powerful influence on the processing of visual information – as well as in other perceptual and cognitive domains. A desk in an office may be expected in almost 100%,– whereas a gorilla waiting for someone in the office is more than unlikely. Familiar objects can often be recognized in the absence of context, but in dealing with less familiar objects, or with complex scenes, or when the viewing conditions are degraded, the role of context increases in importance and can become indispensable. Even when context is not strictly required, the appropriate visual context still facilitates the recognition process, and makes it faster and more reliable [18, 19, 20]. Context information that helps the observer expect a certain class of objects facilitates recognition significantly, and when objects are placed in an unusual context, recognition is hampered. Under natural conditions, useful context information is almost always present, and this accounts in part for our capacity to deal effectively with complex scenes. In artistic pictures this is used to disturb or deceive our expectations, like in the example of the vegetarian head by Arcimboldo (Figure 12).

e. Learning Sequences of Fixations

Recognition in the sequence-seeking scheme can become faster and more efficient by the learning of past successful sequences. A successful sequence is a sequence of pattern activations linking an input pattern with a stored model. When faced again with a similar input, the computation will follow the sequence that proved successful in the past rather than search anew for a possible link between the input and a stored representation. Following practice, out of the huge number of possible sequences those that proved useful in the past will be explored with higher priority in future uses of the viewer. *Searching for the best sequence:* Due to the parallel exploration of multiple alternatives, and to the tuning of the system by past experience, straightforward recognition tasks will require little or no search. More complex tasks will require a search through the space of possible sequences for the appropriate transformations that will bring the viewed object and the stored model into close alignment.

f. Kant's Take on Eye Movement Theory - Visual Processing

Three dichotomies are used in discussing vision. The oldest of these, called the duplicity theory, contrasts foveal and peripheral vision (neurophysiological parallels are X and Y cells, parvo and magnocellular, slow and fast dichotomies). *Foveal* vision supports high resolution recognition with its small field of view, approximately one-half degree, and very high resolution, approximately one-half arc-min (or 20/10 or 120 cycles/degree). Color vision depends upon not only the trichromatic cones of Thomas Young, Maxwell, and Helmholtz, but also on the opponent processing that Hering, Jamison, Hurvich, and DeValois established. Opponent cells are a beautiful example of bottom-up organization of sense data. *Peripheral* vision has a very wide field of view, approximately 120 to 180 degrees, but very low resolution. It is sensitive to motion and flickering lights. Some time ago, the amount of information transmission capability of these two regions was estimated at about 40K bits/second for each aspect of vision. The foveal transmission rate has mainly just noticeable differences of luminance and color contrast for the 2500 foveal pixels. The comparable transmission rate for the periphery arises from the very large number of receptor fields in the wide periphery with perhaps only one bit of information per receptor field [21]. Given the requirement for foveation of any aspect of a picture for which high resolution analysis will occur, continual, very rapid saccadic EM become an essential aspect of ordinary vision. The second dichotomy comes from computer vision, where bottom-up and top down are contrasted. The flow of sensory energy into the early stages of visual processing is bottom-up. The top down aspects are central to the scanpath theory, and have to do with representational cognitive models. These control active-looking as scanpath EM and have to deal with representational cognitive models. The final, third, dichotomy is one proposed by *Kant* having to do with the internal categorization of sensory stimuli as functions of space and time. His "Empfindung" is sensation without space and time, while his notion of perception includes organization in space and time, leaving open the locus for the addition of space-time to sensation.

There are bottom-up organizational processes that attach space and time dimensions to sensation. We prefer to still consider them sensory processing rather than perceptual processing for several reasons. One is that such processes seem to be accomplished by hard-wired networks of neurons that are innate in the various eyes and brains in which they have been studied. Of course, neurophysiologists have assumed bottom-up processing, so their experiments often do not adduce further evidence as to whether these processes are truly bottom-up or top down. A second reason for placing these bottom-up organizational processes with sensation is that perception per se seems to be the place where top down cognitive models are matched and compared with bottom-up information. The matrix for these comparisons seems to be strongly organized already in terms of space and time; for example, the shape from motion studies of Andersen [22, 23].

But does dual vision provide a rationale for the central role of EM? Understanding that visual processes can be bottom-up or top down helps us to put in order our notions about vision. Keep in mind one of the most interesting questions for future neurophysiology, especially aided by active imaging experiments, functional MRI and PET is: "Where does bottom-up vision meet top down vision?" A possible answer is in the loop interactions between layer four (bottom-up) and layer six (top down) in the striate cortex. This site is more likely than loops between geniculate and cortex [24]. Perhaps the "meeting" takes place even later, in the parietal cortex, so devoted to further visual processing, velocity, attention, and interactions with primary motor and motor planning cortical regions [25, 26].

Higher level vision includes perception occurring in the "mind's eye". The cognitive model of a scene or a picture is the philosopher's "representation". Its operational phase is the active-looking scanpath. EM are also driven in a top down fashion so that critical regions of interest,

ROIs, determined from the cognitive model can be sampled with high resolution foveal vision.

The categories of bottom-up and top down do not exactly coincide with Kant's separation of sensation, i.e., empfindung, and perception per se. Physiology has to do with the reception of light in terms of intensity and, more importantly, as contrast – both luminous and color contrast – and also in terms of resolution. Perhaps it is also parallel to Descartes' idea of lux. Here we attempt to reserve Kant's distinction between sensation and perception for the interaction between top down representation and bottom-up sensation, since we employ the scanpath as the operational mode of checking and confirming the top down model in detail with each fixation. A series of bottom-up organizational processes, including Kant's space and time categories, are intermediate.

Wide angle peripheral vision, although of low resolution, is ideally adapted for motion and flow field, and for pre-attentive "pop-up" parallel sensing (perhaps "pre-attentive" is not completely bottom-up). We emphasize that to assess velocity, Kantian categories of time and space must be computed. More recent studies argue in favor of a balanced combination of bottom up and top down processing. Recognition, including the difficult tasks of compensating for the effects of viewing direction, illumination, occlusion and object deformation, can benefit from the use of information associated with objects and object classes, acquired through past experience or as promoting information processing in the visual cortex is therefore the capacity to combine efficiently bottom up processing starting at the image and proceeding to high-level cortical areas, with top down processing, starting at stored object representations, and proceeding from high to low visual areas. The structure of the cortex clearly supports this possibility: a major characteristic of cortical interconnections is the reciprocity of the connections between visual areas. If a visual area in the cortex sends ascending connections to another visual area higher up in the hierarchy of visual processing, then, as a general rule, the second area sends reciprocal connections to the first.

g. Visual Attention and Search Imaging

From the large number of external stimuli that we perceive permanently by the visual, auditory, and somatosensory sense organs and that are transmitted by afferent nerve fiber tracts to our brain, we consciously perceive only few by sorting out those stimuli that are meaningful to us in a given situation. In the somatosensory system, it is well established that gating mechanisms on the spinal, thalamic, and cortical level mediate this selection of information [27, 28, 29]. Roland [30] was the first to show that direction of attention to a certain sensory modality leads to specific patterns of increases of the regional cerebral blood flow (rCBF) in the corresponding primary and secondary receptive cortical areas of the human brain. Here we review neuroimaging studies dealing with attentional processing in the visual domain.

The *visual system* has been demonstrated in subhuman primates to consist of a large number of interconnected striate and extrastriate cortical areas subserving different aspects of visual information processing including an occipito-temporal pathway that is involved in object identification, and an occipito-parietal pathway which mediates the appreciation of spatial relationships among objects. The primate visual cortex can be parcellated into more than 30 cortical visual areas with rich anatomical interconnections. The borders of these areas are not as distinct as in this unfolded map but show transitions and interindividual variabilities. These areas are not fully interconnected but anatomical projections consisting of feed-forward and feed-backward interactions providing different processing levels of a visual cortical hierarchy. This network of cortical areas exceeds the borders of the occipital lobe allowing for communication also with other cortical centers that subserve motor control, other sensory modalities, and supramodal information processing. The reciprocal and recursive connections of the visual network can conceptualize as a system that resolves conflicts between the responses of different areas and constructs new neuronal response properties by the emergence of temporal correlations in the activity of neuronal groups within a cortical area and between different areas.

Vision and its reflection in the mind from a bottom-up perspective

J. W. Goethe related vision and its reflection in the mind from a bottom up perspective. "Seeing is to form a steady, living bond between the eyes of the mind and those the body." The eyes of the body very likely represent low level functions of the visual system. Goethe kept searching for primal states, primal phenomena: the primal plant, primal rock, primal chant, the ultimately simple, the "belief in the originally productive", of which Goethe wrote to Zelter in 1827:

> "These primal phenomena constitute the ultimate experience. They should remain untouched in their eternal repose and glory. For beyond them lies a world that is hidden from us, for which the visible world is only a simile. ... The eye reflects the world on the outside, the man on the inside. The totality of the inner and the outer is perfected in the eye."

Of course, it is not only the bottom up view that is stressed here by Goethe; the idealistic view of primal phenomena that are to be detected by the creative artistic mind is as well important. As he puts it:

> "In nature there is everything that is in the subject and in the subject there is everything that is in nature," describing the exchange of bottom up and top down. The external world is "a reflection responding to one's sentiments", because its "appearance is not detached from the viewer, but rather interwoven with and entangled in his individuality".

Goethe tried to encapsulate this in a schematic formula in his "*Allgemeines Glaubensbekenntnis*" ('*General Creed*') of 1815:
a In nature there is everything that is in the subject
y and something in excess of that
b In the subject there is everything that is in nature
z and something in excess of that

b can recognize a, z can only suspect y
a can be experienced by observation, y cannot
y can be made to be suspected by action

Hence the axiom: "An unknown regularity in the object corresponds to an unknown regularity in the subject." This is about the totality of within and without, which Paul Klee wanted to illustrate for his students by his schematic drawing in *"Wege des Naturstudiums" ('Ways of studying nature')* Figure 13.

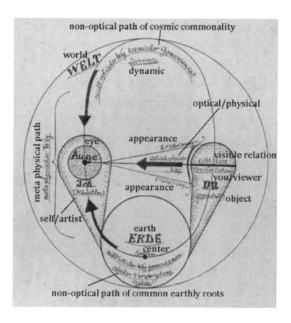

Figure 13. Klee: Wege des Naturstudiums (ca.1923, Feder auf Papier auf Karton, 33x21cm, Zentrum P. Klee, Bern, BG A/29).

"Ways of studying nature" run in three stages:

1st stage: Nature in general as communication with nature, which is indispensable for the artist.

2nd stage: The former setting of the artist to nature was a differentiated exploration of the phenomena in terms of *mimesis theory*. This art of the "optical" vision neglected the art of visualization of non-optical impressions.

3rd stage: The 2nd stage is contrasted with the new concept, in which the artist is not a refined camera but reflects the "inner" of the object. This requires a "totalization" of the view, that is made possible by a process that makes intuitive conclusions of internal processes visible. Non-optical processes are revealed, which leads to a deeper "resonance" of the artist to the subject. There are two ways to get there: Common ground roots and the metaphysical way of cosmic togetherness.

For the more contemporary time of the 20th century we have several comments pointing also in the direction of a higher estimation of peripheral, bottom up vision, like Pierre Bonnard's statement ([31], p.178):

"...the artist is always in danger of allowing himself to be distracted by the effects of direct and immediate vision...., and to lose the primary idea on the way. Thus, after a certain period of work, the painter can no longer recover his original idea and depends on accidental qualities, he reproduces the shadows he sees... and such details as did not strike him at the beginning." Jackson Pollock (interviewed by William Wright, 1950) argued in the same direction: "I think people should not look actively, but look passively –, and try to receive what the painting has to offer and not bring a subject matter or preconceived idea." Pollock is really favoring the low level bottom up viewing with no preconception, which is of course impossible for most viewers. "All cultures have had means and techniques of expressing their immediate aims - the Chinese, the Renaissance, all cultures. The thing that interests me is that today painters do not have to go to a subject matter outside of themselves. Most modern painters work from a different source. They work from within."

This is certainly a very good example how the artist feels his art should be communicated preferably through a bottom up process in order to share the artists experience when he created the work of art using a rather subconscious "psycho-motor" modeling process.

Earlier, Jean Tinguely ([32], p.250) had put forward the paradox argument that movement-transformation-change are to be static and unchanging, and therefore related to the peripheral external world:

"Movement is static because it is the only immutable thing- the only certainty, the only thing that is unchangeable. Immobile, certain, and permanent things, – as ideas, works and beliefs change, transform, and disintegrate. Immobile objects are snapshots of a movement whose existence we refuse to accept, because we ourselves are only an instant in the great movement. Movement is the only static, final, permanent, and certain thing"

Tinguely is in his statement and work close to someone like Pollock, in that he suggests the bottom up sensing of movement and change per se as the only thing we can hold onto. Of course, he also applies his general internal model the permanent changing world onto his works of art: only it is very general and far removed from what we can look at – except for the movement per se.

2. SCANPATH EYE MOVEMENTS

Seeing is top down with the brain, whereas bottom up is seeing with the eyes, plus their interactions. The brain has to create a top down perception of what it expects to see and then actively search the visual world to find confirmation – or rejection – of the percept. The eye has to transmit bottom up signals. In this process, foveal regions-of-interest, ROIs, are sequentially visited by a string of fixations [scanpath], shifted by a string of saccades, rapid eye movements or EM jumps; the foveal ROIs are simultaneously matched by top down, symbolic, spatial and sequential representations, or bindings, of the hypothesized image.

Philosophers had long speculated about perception and how we see in our mind's eye, but little scientific evidence was adduced until the scanpath sequence of eye movements enabled an approach to the problem. The concept of "binding" speaks to the assigning of values for the model and its execution by various parts of the brain. We assume that there are several levels of "binding" – symbolic or semantic binding, spatial binding for the structural locations of the ROIs, and sequential binding for the dynamic execution program that yields the sequence of EM. Searchpaths have a structure similar to scanpaths and are similarly defined as "repetitive, idiosyncratic sequences of saccades alternating with fixations". Their final, efficient EM, foveations and visual processes for recognition and material Aristotelian causes (neurons, nerves, muscles, receptors) are the same. The spatial model for the searchpath includes the geometry of the target loci as its main information content. The spatial model is contrasted with a cognitive model, with cognitive implying some sort of symbolic representation.

An a-priori top–down, cognitive model of the external world is composed of What, Where, and When information which contains conditional probabilities of the elements of the picture. This model controls the scanpath shifts of attention and the iconic matching in the visual cortex between foveated bottom–up visual signals and the top–down model cognitive representation of the foveated object. If image transformations are evoked by motor processes, and if the brain of oneself anticipates what one will see as one moves, then the brain may respect the laws that govern movements, and images will be transformed continuously. We can understand image transformations better, when we analyze sequences of half-blind, hemianopic, patients' EM with string editing and Markov techniques, measured during eye movements viewing real pictures and visual imagery experiments. Results suggested a "convergence of visualization" in all subjects – normal and hemianopic eye movement sequences that were significantly less similar for viewing and re-visualization, but still significantly above the measure of similarity calculated for random sequences, than those for the imageries among each other.

In models of information processing these processes have been specified through the postulation of a sequence of stages between "input" and "output". Eye movement analysis shows that our perceptions are actually constructed from integrating over an extended time many discrete samples of the picture. These models have also been applied to the perception of works of art. Evidence suggests that different styles and periods of art produce different kinds of eye movements and fixations. This was confirmed by the observation that artists intentionally spend more long-to-short gazes (specific to divertive exploration) for the less formal –

less predictable – than the more formal – more predictable – compositional designs, while untrained viewers reiterated the inverse patterns. Trained viewers spent relatively more time in divertive exploration than in specific exploration when viewing the altered pictures, while untrained viewers performed just the opposite.

a. Scanpath – Modes, Experiments, Theory

Seeing is top down with the brain, whereas bottom up is seeing with the eye, plus their interactions. The brain has to create a top down perception of what it expects to see and then actively search the visual world to find confirmation - or rejection - of the percept. The eye has to transmit bottom up signals. The hypotheses of 'top down' and 'bottom-up' can be used with different, but interchangeable meanings, which are given above. The whole concept of top down is more than the idea of feedback signal flow. It encompasses a whole class of phenomena. The above notions of top down are interchangeable, as they partly apply at different levels of description. The essential problem is how to match bottom-up with top down; the bottom up confirmatory signals coming both from the wide peripheral visual field with low level vision, which has only low resolution but with high sensitivity for moving objects, and from multiple high-resolution samples and glimpses by the centrally located fovea, a small, circa one-degree region. These foveal regions-of-interest, ROIs, are sequentially visited by a string of fixations, shifted by a string of saccades, rapid eye movements or EM jumps; the foveal ROIs are simultaneously matched by top down, symbolic, spatial and sequential representations, or bindings, of the hypothesized image.

When the retinal field is mapped onto the occipital primary visual cortex, there is a considerable geometrical magnification of the signals coming from the fovea, and a consequent reduction of signals coming from the periphery. A log-polar distortion (Figure 14) is a rather good depiction of the geometry of the visual image mapped onto the visual cortex. When the high-resolution fovea is fixated on a particular part of the picture, such as the face of a human character, a shoe or an animal, that ROI is magnified on the visual cortex. Contrariwise, those parts of the image lying on the periphery of the retina are minimized, so that only color and textural segmentation of large areas can be appreciated at the low resolution of the periphery. Such foveal and peripheral representations (Figure 14) provide an indication of the kind of bottom up information coming into the visual brain.

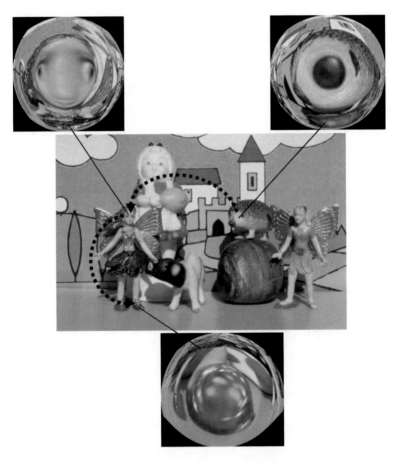

Figure 14. Space-variant vision.

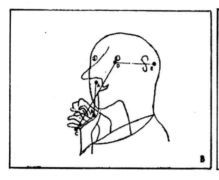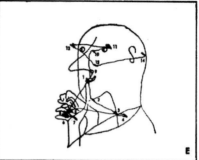

Figure 15. Top-down Scanpath EM viewing a Paul Klee picture [33].

Top-down involves the brain taking part in "active looking", by which the brain frames a complex hypothesis of what is "out there" based on a priori knowledge, peripheral patches of texture, color, motion, depth, and then uses the scanpath eye movement sequence strategy to search out and import information to confirm - or reject - the current guess or hypothesis.

Philosophers had long speculated about perception and how we see in our mind's eye, but little scientific evidence was adduced until the scanpath sequence of eye movements enabled an approach to the problem. The scanpath sequence itself, consists of alternating saccadic eye movements, EM, and fixations that enable the active-looking paradigm. The controlling top down model has its roots in philosophy. For more than 2000 years, thoughtful scholars have considered the relationships possible between inner awareness and conscious perception, most likely not all iconic. Perception can check by iconic matching to physical signals arriving to the brain via peripheral nerves and sensory organs. The earliest experiments showed the sequential and repetitive character of the scanpath and its idiosyncratic nature with respect to the person viewing and the picture or scene viewed. These experiments suggested the reality of the scanpath EM sequence for several kinds of static pictures. However, most scenes are dynamic. Thus, a test of the scanpath theory would be to ask whether EM, while looking at such dynamic scenes, could be similarly characterized as a scanpath sequence. Ambiguous and fragmented figures shift in their visual perceptions [34]; so do the scanpaths traced over the constant physical picture. Thus, they appear to be generated from an internal model or schema rather than being controlled by external visual world signals impinging upon the brain. Quite a few laboratories have confirmed these results (see references below); also, one can go back to precursor static experiments like those of Yarbus and Buswell (see Introduction – Figures 3 and 4) to see evidence of the repetitive sequences we call the scanpaths.

The philosophers from Plato onwards have thought deeply about these matters, and we have tried to summarize their views (Figure 16). This five-component visual perceptual schema has been obtained by using four terms defined by the philosopher Kant. We start with the world of appearances, known as the "chaos" to early Greek philosophers; in our terminology, it is called "bottom-up stuff". At one time, we used "thing" for the so-called "real" outside world, but someone pointed out that by the time the brain had done figure-ground separation and knew about the physical coherence of objects, much of the perception of the world had already been accomplished. The next stage, sensation, represents the inflows of energy onto body sensoria. It now appears that the filtering expected by Muller for "specific nerve energies" is actually accomplished by "specific nerve endings". We call the next stage, sensory organization, bottom-up physiology, without the Kantian internal constructs of space and time. The frog's eye, using bug detectors, can calculate the velocity of a small moving spot accurately enough to have kept frogs very well in bugs for the last 350 million years of vertebrate evolution. It took 350 million years of cellular evolution to arrive at the frog's eye, and another 350 million years to arrive at the brains of McCulloch and Lettvin [35], so that they were capable of demonstrating the elegance of this aspect of the sensory organization of the frog's eye.

Since velocity requires both space and time computation, it is clear that these bottom-up processes have been captured by evolution. If we jump ahead to representation, the "ideals" of Plato and the "notions" of Berkeley, we see that our term, "top down cognitive models", can perhaps be symbolized with a file drawer icon. We will return to the question of representation in the third subsection below. Such models, acting top down onto the fourth column, perception per se, can be seen to be planned, forceful, determined sets of activities. In our model for perception, the top down active looking scanpath plays its role as the operational phase of perception per se. This set of five columns, decomposing the perceptual process taken overall, leads to an important question we can pose for the neurophysiologist, "Where does top down meet bottom-up?" Our answer is where top down inputs to levels I, II, and III of the visual cortex meet bottom-up visual signal information going to levels IV and V in the retinotopic visual cortex.

How is the internal model distributed and operationally assembled? The concept of binding (Figure 17) speaks to the assigning of values for the model and its execution by various parts of the brain. We assume that there are several levels of "binding" – symbolic or semantic binding, spatial binding for the structural locations of the ROIs, and sequential binding for the dynamic execution program that yields the sequence of EM. We also try to use current neurological information to localize where these different aspects of the spatial-cognitive model might exist in the brain.

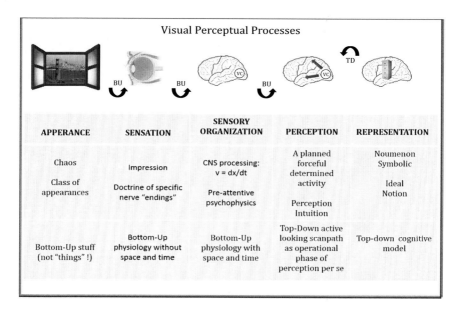

Figure 16. World of appearances - Visual Perceptual Processes.

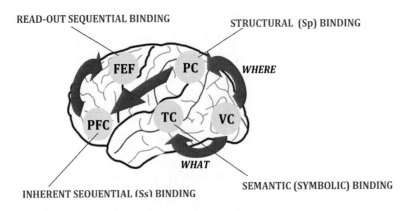

Figure 17. Binding and the modular cortex. Four general possibilities of binding [sequential, symbolic, geometric and structural], and also hypothetical regions of the cortex, where this might happen according to evidence from studies over the last 15 years. Arrows show the specific interconnections with respect to the visual system [34].

The effect of spatial and temporal information on saccades and neural activity in oculomotor structures shows that the neural structures supporting the "where" and "when" systems are highly overlapping. Knowledge of timing and target direction converge in the precentral gyrus, a region where there is strong evidence of context-dependent modulation of neural activity [36].

The scanpath was defined on the basis of experimental findings. It consists of sequences of alternating saccades and fixations that repeat themselves when a subject is viewing a picture, scene or object (Figure 18). Only ten percent of the duration of the scanpath is taken up by the collective durations of the saccadic EM; the intervening fixations or foveations make up ninety percent of the total viewing period, providing an efficient mechanism for traveling over the scene or picture of interest [1, 9, 37, 38]. Scanpath sequences appeared spontaneously without special instructions to subjects and were next discovered to be repetitive and idiosyncratic to a particular picture and to a particular subject [12, 13]. However, they could be shifted somewhat by different instructions or by implicitly assumed task conditions, confirming Yarbus' (1967) pioneering work [11] using static displays of EM (also [7, 8, 10, 39]. This early evidence indicated that the scanpath was not only idiosyncratic to a particular subject but was also strongly related to the loci of important picture information in a particular picture or scene - the regions of interest (ROIs).

The early experiments suggested to Noton and Stark that an internal cognitive model drove the EM in the repetitive scanpath sequence. A more complete statement of the scanpath theory asserts that the internal cognitive model controls not only the active-looking scanpath EM, but also the perceptual process itself, during which the foveations permit checking and confirming the sub-features of the cognitive model; thus, human visual perception is largely a top down process [12, 13, 34].

The symbolic representations, or cognitive models, of a face and hands and of "this" face and hands, together with confirmation from the sparse sampling in time and space to which successive foveations contribute, provide the remarkably vivacious illusion of "clarity and completeness" characteristic of ordinary vision. The scanpath can be considered the sparse operational readout of the symbolic representation. Instructions for a scanpath include subfeatures and directions for travels from one subfeature to the next, yet even together they do not make up an iconic representation. Higher level vision includes perception occurring in the "mind's eye", where the cognitive model of a scene or a picture is the philosopher's "representation". Its operational phase is the active-looking scanpath. EM are also driven in a top down fashion so that critical ROIs determined from the cognitive model can be sampled with high resolution foveal vision.

Before using the methods for evaluation of the view of an image, the images must be divided into ROIs (Figure 19) and every ROI was assigned a letter. This ROI division is the most common method for comparing image viewing. So, each view is characterized with one string of letters. Afterwards, these strings could be analyzed by the methods described below, using the a prior and a posteriori ROI definition.

In the next Figure 20 the principally possible scanpath distributions have been simulated by a Markov model: left deterministic, middle probabilistic, right random.

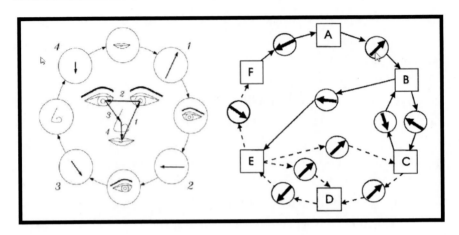

Figure 18. Scanpath sequence of a face, starting from upper lip to left eye (modif. from [40] with permission). Left: the basic scanpath sensory-motor cycle. Right: A more realistic less abstracted version with jumps from E to C, or B to E.

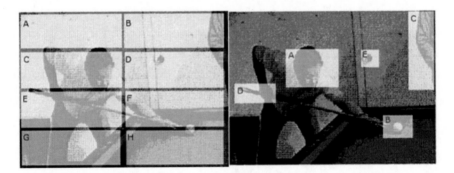

Figure 19. ROI definition. Left: a priori ROI definition representing geometric ROIs. Right: semantic a posteriori ROI definition representing subfeatures of the scene defined by the experimentator.

The early evidence of the repetitive and idiosyncratic nature of the scanpath suggested, but did not prove, that an internal cognitive model controlled the scanpath EM sequences. The new evidence extends these findings with objective statistical *string editing* similarity measures. In addition to older work showing that the scanpath changes with shifts in the subject's mental image, there is now evidence that the scanpath during *visual imagery* is quite similar to the scanpath while viewing. Without any external world, the internal cognitive mode must be the source of the structure of the scanpath in these visual imagery experiments [40, 41].

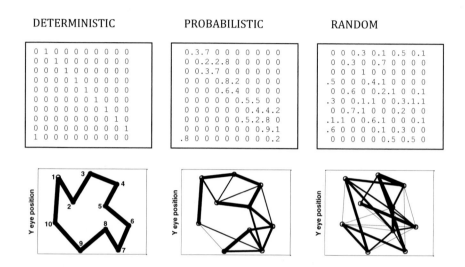

DETERMINISTIC

```
0 1 0 0 0 0 0 0 0 0
0 0 1 0 0 0 0 0 0 0
0 0 0 1 0 0 0 0 0 0
0 0 0 0 1 0 0 0 0 0
0 0 0 0 0 1 0 0 0 0
0 0 0 0 0 0 1 0 0 0
0 0 0 0 0 0 0 1 0 0
0 0 0 0 0 0 0 0 1 0
0 0 0 0 0 0 0 0 0 1
1 0 0 0 0 0 0 0 0 0
```

PROBABILISTIC

```
0 .3 .7 0  0  0  0  0  0  0
0 0 .2 .8  0  0  0  0  0  0
0 0 .3 .7  0  0  0  0  0  0
0 0 0  0  .8 .2 0  0  0  0
0 0 0  0  .6 .4 0  0  0  0
0 0 0  0  0  0 .5 .5 0  0
0 0 0  0  0  0  0 .4 .4 .2
0 0 0  0  0  0 .5 .2 .8 0
0 0 0  0  0  0  0  0 .9 .1
.8 0 0 0  0  0  0  0  0 .2
```

RANDOM

```
0  0  0 0.3 0.1 0 0.5 0.1
0  0.3 0 0.7 0  0  0  0
0  0  0  1  0  0  0  0  0  0
.5 0  0 0.4 .1 0  0  0  0
0  0.6 0 0.2 .1 0  0.1
.3 0 0.1 .1 0 0.3 .1 .1
0 0.7 .1 0  0 0.2 0  0
.1 .1 0 0.6 .1 0 0 0.1
.6 0  0  0 0.1 0.3 0  0
0  0  0  0  0 0.5 0.5 0
```

Figure 20. Simulated scanpaths with Markov matrices.

b. Cognitive Spatial Models for Search

Searchpaths have a structure similar to scanpaths and are similarly defined as "repetitive, idiosyncratic sequences of saccades alternating with fixations". Their final, efficient EM, foveations and visual processes for recognition and material Aristotelian causes (neurons, nerves, muscles, receptors) are the same. However, they are different in that they are generated and controlled by spatial models and not by the rich and compacted structure of the symbolic cognitive models that generate and control scanpaths; their formal causes are different: They have different properties of the spatial model versus those of the cognitive model. Many findings suggest that spatial models represent the ability to remember positions of about six to seven loci, ROIs containing objects or subfeatures of interest. When the number of loci increases significantly above 10 then the spatial model cannot handle this complexity and thus cannot accurately generate repetitive patterns from locus to locus. The only solution is to treat these large numbers of loci as a random search scene and to develop a "cover" algorithm so as not to miss portions of the search area [42, 43]. However, if the loci are organized into an object, a pattern, or a series of subfeatures in a meaningful picture, then a cognitive model can be addressed, if it already exists; or a new one can be constructed by analogic reasoning. With this cognitive model, the brain can operate in the recognition area, generate a scanpath and confirm a percept at one and the same time.

The spatial model for the searchpath includes the geometry of the target loci as its main information content. The spatial model is contrasted with a cognitive model, with cognitive implying some sort of symbolic representation. The subfeatures of a searchpath model are identical and require a single matched filter or some equivalent for the set of 7 +/- 2 identical targets in the different loci. These are subfeatures indeed, since search requires detection, recognition and identification. However, the information they contribute is less than the linkage information, and is identical for each class of target and decoy.

c. Vision without a Cognitive Spatial Model?

The simplest vision experiment is perhaps to present a flash of light to the peripheral retina in a dark room, and then to measure the EM the subject directs to that location. To the naive realist, this appears to be a clear-cut case of the external world controlling EM, and a clear counter-example to the scanpath. Two different considerations demonstrate that this simple view is not likely to be true. If one puts lenses or prisms on the subject's eyes, the subject will make errors in fixating the flashed locus and will then have to adapt his ocular-motor-spatial model or frame-of-reference [44]. This is telling evidence that such a spatial model or frame-of-reference must exist for the initial simple experiment.

d. Scanpath Eye Movements as Indicators of Mental Operations

It is interesting to note that some psychological schools tend more to stress the difficulties when dealing with the subject of eye movements and cognition, whereas others try to abstract the sheer individuality of eye movement patterns and cognition in favor of distinctly selected topics. Attempts have been made to use eye movements as indicators of mental operations for more than a century [45] (however with criticisms [46]). Such attempts were often unsuccessful. They shed little light on cognitive processes, in part because eye movement patterns vary greatly among, individuals, tasks and even within the same individual and task. Difficulties, however, go beyond issues of variability. In order to infer mental operations from eye movements, it has been necessary to make a number of assumptions. One of these assumptions is that locus of fixation indicates either: (i) the place in the visual field that contains the information that is being processed mentally, or (ii) the particular type of mental operation taking place, e.g., comparing object colors vs. object shapes in a matching task. Another assumption (iii) is that the amount of time spent looking at a particular locus is proportional to the amount of mental processing of information at that locus [47]. These assumptions, although frequently made, are difficult to verify because mental processing is private and cannot be measured directly.

Despite the fact that before the arrival of the scanpath theory and its later experimental confirmation, attempts to determine moment-by-moment mental operations by looking at individual eye movements have been problematic – examining global patterns of eye movements have yielded some interesting and useful insights into the mental world of subjects in visuomotor experiments.

Ballard et al. [48, 49] for example, found that when subjects were asked to copy meaningless shapes made by arranging an assembly of colored blocks, they looked at the shape to be copied an average of twice for each block they arranged, at least while they were arranging the first three blocks. This strategy was pervasive and suggested that, at least in this type of task, the subjects were using the visible display as an extension of their memory. Rather than memorizing the locations of several blocks at a time the subjects chose to look at the model repeatedly while the copy was built. This strategy changed when eye movements were made more expensive by placing the model farther away from the work area within which the copy was being built. In this case subjects did not look at the model as often, and used their memory more.

When eye and head movements were recorded as unrestrained subjects tapped or only looked at nearby targets, scanning patterns were the same in both tasks: subjects looked at each target before tapping it; visual search had similar speeds and gaze-shift accuracies. Looking, however, took longer and, unlike tapping, benefitted little from practice. Looking speeded up more than tapping when memory load was reduced: memory was more efficient during tapping. Eye movements made when only looking are different from those made when tapping. Therefore, visual search functions as a separate process, incorporated into both tasks can be used to improve performance when memory load is heavy.

e. The Privitera-Stark Model

A general Bayesian framework of bottom–up-conspicuity and top–down-informativeness eye movements control has been proposed more recently by Privitera and Stark [50]. An a-priori top–down, cognitive model of the external world is composed of What, Where, and When information which contains conditional probabilities of the elements of the picture. This model controls the scanpath shifts of attention (eye movement sequence, bottom panel) and the iconic matching in the visual cortex between foveated bottom–up visual signals and the top–down model cognitive representation of the foveated (F) object O^F. Low resolution conspicuity (C) matching, O^C is also necessary. The result of the matching is given as feedback to the top–down representation to confirm or correct the internal visual hypothesis. The top–down cognitive-spatial model contains a knowledge representation of the elements in the background setting of the picture, the corresponding conditional probability (What), of the loci (Where), and of the sequences (When).

A scene hypothesis is formulated based on the matching of low-resolution (peripheral) conspicuity (analog expression to saliency) objects, O^Cs. These objects can be identified with the conspicuity operators, which represent specific spatial and geometric features belonging to the visual scene. Other bottom-up operators, color for example, might be more appropriate for other images or visual tasks and combined with the geometric operators. A priori knowledge in the form of conditional probabilities between the hypothesis and the complete foveated object is used to make saccades more accurate in their generation in their attempt to capture, match and thus check on complete, most informative, foveal objects, O^F. Every time the fovea is placed on one of these objects (O^F), bottom-up visual signals in log polar retinotopic iconic form arrive via the retina and lateral geniculate nuclei to layers IV and V of the visual cortex (Figure 21, middle panel, iconic matching). These icons are sequentially, and probably hierarchically, matched with the cognitive-spatial representations projected top–down from other cortical areas. Matching of low-resolution peripheral conspicuity regions (Figure 21), middle panel, peripheral image acquisition) is important to inform the planning control and help manage internal representation. Matching confirmation results of these hypothesized icons thus either support the ongoing overall perception or contribute to the creation of a new hypothesis. Here is the entire confirmatory scanpath process in an algorithmic format:

Step 1: Various forms of conspicuity objects O^Cs are analyzed from a low-resolution inspection of the visual stimulus. They can be specific spatial operators, such as geometrical kernels, and/or other bottom-up conspicuities such as color;

Step 2: Create an initial scene hypothesis (What and Where) based on these conspicuity objects O^Cs. For example small triangular patterns on a blue background or vertical dark bars on a yellow background can identify a natural beach scene with sailboats on the ocean and people strolling on the sand;

Step 3: Assign a saliency to each conspicuity based on the contribution of the corresponding object to the picture.

Step 4: Fixate the center of the object with the highest saliency that has not yet been fixated (When). The icon matching of complete foveal objects O^Fs serves to strengthen – or weaken – the probability of the hypothesis;

Step 5: Repeat Step 4 until verification is complete or start again from Step 1 with a new hypothesis if verification is not achieved. The same mechanism is applicable if the picture is only imagined – see next section.

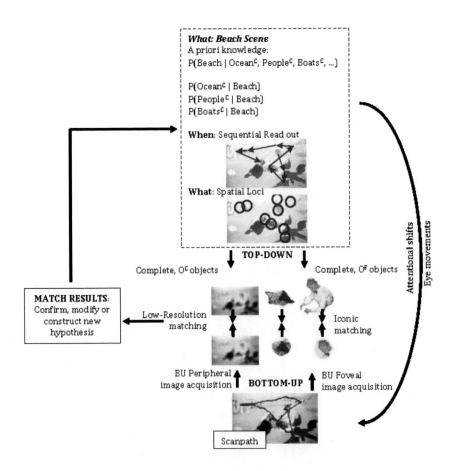

Figure 21. Privitera Stark model (2005): see text for explanation.

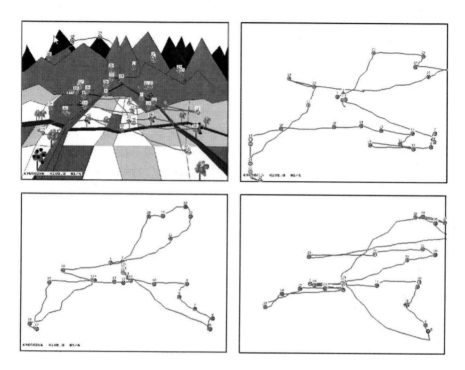

Figure 22. Demonstration of scanpath responses to real and imagined stimuli (from [40]). Compare the similarity of left and right scanpaths on left picture, and on right picture (clockwise). Similarities between consecutive eye movement sequences showed a significant decrease between viewing and the first imagery, whereas between the last two imageries only comparatively slight increases in similarity showed up. These matching results for normal subjects and hemianopic patients suggest a strong top down component in viewing an image with a cognitive model of the image viewed constructed very early in the viewing process, which controls the eye movements during viewing and imagining as well.

f. Visual Imagery and Scanpath Eye Movements

During perception, the shape shift subsystem [51] systematically alters representations of the spatiotopic mapping and alters the imagery mapping function. During imagery, the priming causes an image to form, and as the shape shift subsystem alters spatial representations it alters the mapping from the pattern activation to the visual buffer to be consistent with the new spatial properties. If image transformations are evoked by motor processes, and if the brain of oneself anticipates what one will see as one moves, then the brain may respect the laws that govern movements, and images will be transformed continuously. Concerning visual imagery, Kamiya [52] has suggested that the relationship between eye movements and mental activity might be more profitably examined in the waking state. In normal subjects a one-to-one relation between REM (rapid eye movements during sleep) and dreaming was not observed. Reliable self-reporting of dream pictures is difficult to achieve and therefore a qualitative comparison to REM seems impossible. Accordingly, a different approach using psychophysical methods shed more light on the spatial characteristics of mental images. Scanning times were used as a measure for spatial distance between points in the visualized image [53, 54]. The scanning times were found to be linearly correlated with the spatial distance between points in the mental image, a finding that supported Kosslyn's theory [55] of a visual working memory with intrinsic two-dimensional properties. Experiments with Necker cubes [56] suggested that the output of the memory representation has a three-dimensional structure, even when viewing two-dimensional drawings. Mental rotation of three-dimensional objects [57, 58] also revealed spatial properties for visual imagery that are analogous to visual perception. Experiments showing that imagery can cause illusions and after-effects normally caused by visual perception [59] support the claim that imagery is not just spatial, but specifically visual. Brandt and Stark [41] have analyzed eye movement patterns during imagery and correlated the distribution of fixations and saccades with the visual content of the mental image and with the eye movement patterns when viewing the picture that had to be imagined. Similarities and differences were determined quantitatively using string editing algorithms. In the viewing condition the distribution of fixations reflected the distribution of the shaded areas of an abstract pattern. The same was true for the distribution of fixations in the imagery conditions. If the eye movements during the imagery period of the experiment were not random but indeed reflected the content of the visualized diagram, then any eye movement patterns recorded during imagery should be more similar to the corresponding viewing pattern of eye movements than to any other eye movement pattern obtained from different stimulus rotations. The string editing analysis proved quantitatively this hypothesis. It confirmed the high degree of similarity in the recorded eye movements between the viewing period and the imagery period.

Sequences of half-blind, hemianopic patient's EM were analyzed with string editing and Markov techniques (Figure 22 [60, 40]). They measured eye movements during viewing of real pictures and during visual imagery experiments. Subjects were shown an image on a computer screen for a duration of 10 sec; five, thirty, and sixty sec later they were asked to re-visualize the image on the screen. To evaluate the eye movement sequences observed during the original viewing and in the imageries, they used measures of similarity and Markov analyses. Their results suggested a "convergence of visualization" in all subjects - normal and hemianopic eye movement sequences were significantly less similar for viewing and re-visualization, but still significantly above the measure of similarity calculated for random sequences, than those for the imageries among each other.

g. Comparison of Scanpaths While Viewing Realistic and Abstract Art in Normal Subjects and Hemianopic Patients

Repetitive sequences of saccadic EM, i.e., scanpaths occurred when normal healthy subjects viewed slide projections of both realistic and abstract art. Variance analysis demonstrated that global/local eye movement indices were lower for local scanning by professional art viewers who relied on more global viewing, particularly in abstract images. Non-professional, unsophisticated subjects carried their local scanpath patterns from realistic images on to abstract images. The blink rate of professional subjects viewing abstract images was also significantly lower, indicating increased visual effort. Non-professional viewers showed no difference in blink rates (Figure 23 [61]).

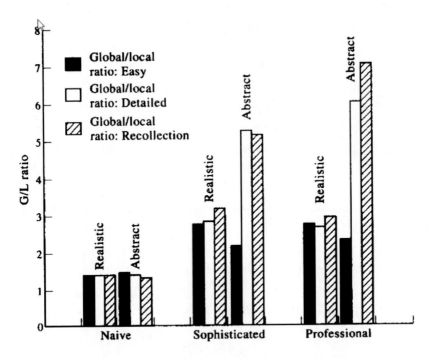

Figure 23. Statistical comparison between professional, sophisticated, naïve viewers while viewing realistic and abstract art in normal subjects. Ratio of global to local amount of scanning (G/L) of naïve, professional and sophisticated viewers of artful pictures that were either "abstract" or "realistic". Note that the more professional viewers showed much higher global/local ratios, especially when viewing abstract pictures in both conditions, detailed and recollection [61]

Since the underlying hypothesis for the scanpath theory is that an internalized cognitive model drives the eye movements, then from this observational evidence we inferred that in our experiments such models drive the eye movement patterns similarly for both healthy and patient subjects searching and scanning realistic, ambiguous and abstract pictures. Therefore, the cognitive model should guide the eye movements in every condition, i.e., scanpath eye movements should occur also in searching and scanning towards the side of the blind hemifield of the hemianopic patient.

Indeed, during viewing realistic as well as abstract pictures, a particular pattern of eye movements occurred according to the relative percentage of time the eye movements spent in making a global scan versus a local scan, using smaller eye movements in a particular region, depending if the patients looked to the seeing or to the blind side of their hemifield. These observations were confirmed by the evaluation of the global/local (G/L) ratio of each subject for each picture and task. A clear cut difference was also demonstrated in the much higher G/L ratio of healthy as compared to the patient viewers when looking at abstract images especially in the search task [60].

A second result of our studies was the relatively high frequency of local scanning when patients viewed the complex visual test stimuli. Evidently, global viewing is the preferred strategy for the healthy subject who tries to evaluate both at the same time the visual content and the complexity of the picture. The patients with visual field deficits however, were busier developing a more optimal sequence of eye movements to detect the overall features of the picture when searching or scanning, since they primarily had to rely on more local and therefore limited picture evaluations that also included more bottom-up control than in the healthy subjects.

What is local scanning? Although Noton and Stark [12], and Stark and Ellis [62] showed that peripheral information can be excluded as the immediate control for the scanpath, their results also relate to local scanpaths. Groner [63] and Finke [64] support their top down, cognitive model scanpath theory for a global scanpath, but argue in favor of an immediate peripheral bottom-up control of local scanning as Grossberg [65] does, although evidence for the latter is not conclusive at the present time. Although interesting, it is quite difficult to demonstrate conclusive evidence of a mini- or micro- search/scan-path as a special case of a local scanpath in hemianopic patients [40].

When viewing a painting, artists perceive more and different information from the painting on the basis of their experience and knowledge than art naïve subjects do, especially when the painting contains no figurative objects, i.e., is an abstract painting [66]. N Koide et al. [67] compared the distribution of eye fixations of artists and naïve subjects during viewing of various abstract paintings using a topological attentional map that quantified the conspicuity of low-level features in the painting, i.e., a saliency map. Fixation distributions of artists viewing abstract paintings differed significantly more from the saliency map than that of naïve subjects. This difference indicates that fixations of artists are less driven by low-level features from bottom-up than naïve viewers. Rather, artists may extract visual information from paintings based on high-level features that they detect following their individual top down model due to professional studies.

Jeannerod [68] has argued for an exchange between local and global scanning in free exploration, as in the *Rorschach* task. Evidently, the normal healthy viewer avoids this type of immediate bottom-up control in favor of the top down controlled global scanpath, whereas the patient when viewing to the side of the blind hemifield relies strongly on such an exchange, which permits him to develop a more efficient strategy of searching and scanning with almost every repetition. This change with repetition is gradual and progressive in patients, whereas we would expect it to be a brisk change (switch) in normal subjects with a digitally simulated hemianopic field defect. This has been shown by Zangemeister and Oechsner [69] and Zangemeister and Utz [70] using an experimental paradigm that utilized short term adaptation to a virtual hemianopia.

Our paradigms for viewing realistic and non-realistic images probably enforced this ability that was not present in the patient viewers. There, the naive subjects had equal global/local ratios for both realistic and abstract images. These ratios were similar to that of sophisticated subjects that were trained to look at art viewing realistic images. Whether the local scanpath is driven immediately by peripheral, bottom-up information or by small-scale cognitive models remains unknown. Locher and Nodine [71] claimed immediate bottom up control in symmetry "that catches the eye"; Mackworth and Morandi [72] showed evidence for top down active selection of informative details through active gaze. In any case, this detailed looking is apparently usual for realistic images, where anticipation of details may be balanced by a permanent exchange of bottom-up and top down control. The patients carry this behavior to the ambiguous and non-realistic images. They use a more bottom-up like strategy when they first view pictures that extend also in to their blind hemifield [73]. Only after many repetitions do they apply a more top down like strategy that mirrors the one they use primarily when looking towards their seeing hemifield.

The artist paints a thing in order to see – aesthetic experience has its roots in totemism

Claude Levi Strauss thought that "the artist paints a thing in order to see" that is with the aesthetic knowledge or imaginative experience which is the work of art – similarly as Paul Klee who said "art does not represent the world, it makes things visible".

Linguistically, art's effectiveness depends upon its surface *vagueness*, which is not meant in the sense of a lack of focus, but rather in the artist's success in shifting our minds from an empirical level of comprehension to the mythic. So the artist's model prescribes an oscillation, or many shifts that open up the viewer's maybe so far "static" model, to become "oscillatory" and therefore able to communicate with the artist. Also, this process may be independent of the historical time gap between viewer and artist, although this gap may be very often a point of great misunderstanding. In his view art is simultaneously connected to two systems: The first is based on a viewer's capacity to organize his experiences, i.e., to shape his model to his synchronous needs, while viewing and contemplating the works of art. The second is a learned system of plastic codes of meaning. The artist manipulates signs into various new permutations. So, what we refer to as "aesthetic experience" has its roots in totemism:

"Totems define rules of behaviour defined in the properties of totemic relationships." One of the characteristics of myths is that they seem to promise rules of order but not deliver them."

Undoubtedly conscious knowledge of the rules of art would dispel the illusion of art at once, since these deal with unconscious mechanisms concerning the use of objects, materials, and concepts in mediating reality, namely in defining the artist's relationships to nature and culture:

> "These relationships are only tangentially concerned with physical properties of the art object, that is, its formal content. As proved in the last few decades, art may assume almost any form or be made in any way; the facturing process is not any more central to the creation of art. Yet the structural significance of the fabricating process vis-a-vis time and the consistency of what is selected is immensely important".

Again, Levy-Strauss describes the top down principle of visual cognition while viewing art. When we look at a normal representation, there is nothing to prevent us from forming a hypothesis about the figure ground relationship or about the way the shapes add up to pictures of objects, like in our example from Cy Twombly, Figure 24, where we may ask ourselves what this kind of "notes" might mean.

Figure 24. Cy Twombly: "Untitled (Roman Notes)" 1970.

Realistic versus non-realistic, and ambiguous pictures – the "filling in". Healthy subjects demonstrated more global scanning of the ambiguous and non-realistic images than they showed for their scanning of the realistic images, as was expected from earlier results. These differences showed up not only in the significantly increased G/L ratios, but also directly in the scanpath patterns of the eye movements when fixation frequency, duration and interfixational saccadic amplitudes were compared. Hemianopic patients, however, first showed sequences of small amplitude fixational saccades as a local scanpath in both visual hemifields, i.e., they searched for some primarily relevant detail by use of which they could then generate a global scanpath. During this phase, their sequences of eye fixations appeared to be bottom-up influenced. Only after several repetitions were they able to change to the more efficient global scanpath while perceiving the different faces of the ambiguous figure, preferably on the side of the seeing hemifield, and rarely also on the side of the blind hemifield. In case of comparatively small visual field defects due to retinal scotoma the question is: how could the cortical reorganization due to a binocular retinal scotoma function? A possible solution is that the neurons in higher cortical areas receiving the signal from the reorganized V1 [primary visual] region interpret it according to the original retinotopic map and treat it as if the signal originated from visual input within the scotoma as proposed by Gilbert [74] and also Ramachandran [75]. The subject would perceive as though the visual features present at the surround of the scotoma also exist within the scotoma. Such mislocalization of visual signals might cause perceptual filling-in at the binocular scotoma, Figure 25.

Evidence for top down versus bottom-up control was given with respect to seeing versus blind hemifield, demonstrating the paradox that top down cognitive models prevail when we see (seeing hemifield), whereas local (stair-)steps of bottom-up controlled EM prevail when we are blind (blind hemifield). We found a strategy of improvement with repetition [69], and the "complexity" of the picture [76] that influences the control of eye movement sequences of fixations. The task could induce more global top down control and influence the size of the region that is viewed (region of interest, ROI) prescribing the type of control that is applied: global versus local scanpath. This study demonstrated that it was feasible and quantifiable to observe short-term adaptation as an effect of short-term training in patients with hemianopic field defects who apply and optimize a high level, top down visuo-motor strategy to search and scan for targets and sequences of targets in complex visual tasks.

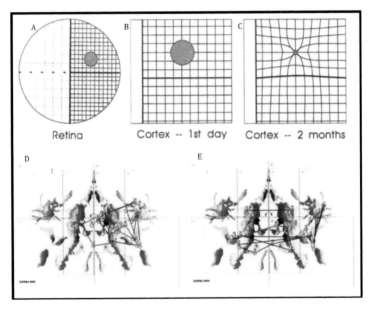

Figure 25. Cortical reorganization due to retinal scotoma (upper).
Schematic illustration of the reorganization of the retinotopic map of the visual cortex following a binocular retinal lesion. A. Schematic illustration of a retinal lesion (gray patch) on the visual field map (grid) projected onto the retina. A retinal lesion at the same visual field location is also made in the opposite eye. B. Retinotopic map of the visual cortex immediately after the binocular retinal lesion. A silent region appears (gray patch) that corresponds to the binocular scotoma, and neurons in this region are not responsive to any visual stimuli. No clear distortion of the retinotopic map is observed. C. Retinotopic map of the visual cortex several months after the retinal lesion. Neurons in the originally silenced region are responsive to stimuli presented around the scotoma, and there is clear distortion of the retinotopic map. Parts A–C modified, with permission, from Gibert 1993 [74].
Looking for a hidden face (lower). Before (left) and after training (right) of a patient who is blind on her left hemifield viewing an ambiguous picture (from [60]).

Perceptual anticipation, looking again and filling in

Unless we are looking straight at that tree, it is not represented in any detail in our visual system, the representation having been washed away at the last EM saccade.

It only appears to be available to consciousness because we can look again. This reveals an important distinction between the "presence of representation" and the "representation of presence". The fact that sometimes we confuse these two contributes to an illusion. The questions which arise from here are: How does the visual system detect changes in the environment and how much information is retained at each saccade? How much missing detail is "filled in" by the cognitive system (Figure 26) [77, 75]. If the "looking again" strategy is to succeed, it may rely on the external world remaining stable across the time required to change fixation – to "look again". Since this time is relatively short the visual system may be able to get away with it. During a single fixation, the visual system is highly sensitive to many kinds of spatial, temporal, and chromatic changes in the visual input. This high sensitivity to change is supported by several special mechanisms, e.g., retinal adaptation [78], the "pop-out" system [79], and motion detectors [80]. It is this special sensitivity to change during each fixation that gives us an inflated impression of our awareness of change between fixations? There is an odd implication of this view – that changes occurring between fixations should not be easily detectable. In other words, little information need be retained from one saccade to the next. Psychophysical evidence shows that images function as perceptual "anticipations" – imagining an object would speed up perception by initiating the appropriate perceptual processes in advance [81, 82]. By imagining letters of the alphabet (H and T) that match presented letters, the ability to detect the letter induced a threshold reduction of 50% as compared with perception; the imagery – induced facilitation was specific to the orientation of the stimulus.

The subjects were more accurate in detecting the letters, in which detection was performed without imagery. However, the facilitation effect was probably due to a spatially localized shift of criterion rather than to a change in sensitivity. Thus, facilitation may reflect processes other than changes in visual sensitivity. Imagery-induced interference and facilitation appear to be memory-dependent: Visual recall of common objects from long-term memory can interfere with perception, while on short-term memory tasks facilitation can be obtained.

Figure 26. Filling in perception, Magritte, Carte Blanche, 1956.

This supports the distinction between low-level and structural representations in visual memory. Therefore, the existence of a stimulus specific short term memory system that stores the visual sensory-motor trace and enables reactivation of pictorial representations by top down processes appears to be the likely explanation, i.e., the scanpath feature ring. Stimulus parameters appear to dominate the imagery induced facilitation at short target-to-mask distances, whereas the top down component contributes to the effect at long target-to-mask distances. Concerning art perception and imagery it has been shown that repeated imagery after very short picture presentation leads to a slow decrease of characteristic scanpath eye movements that were initially very similar to the recordings during the perception of the real paintings.

h. Eye Movement Analysis as Key to Understanding Aesthetic Processes

Eye movement analysis shows that our perceptions are actually constructed from integrating over an extended time many discrete samples of the picture. The fact that visual attention is biased towards certain "informative" parts of the pictures (ROI) is indicative of processes of inference and of guidance of sequences of fixations. In models of information processing these processes have been specified through the postulation of a sequence of stages between "input" and "output". These models have also been applied to the perception of works of art. Marschalek for example [83], has discussed developmental changes in aesthetic responses in terms of stages of attention, perceptual memory, short-term memory, and processing capacity. The cognitive approach to the perception of pictures means: it emphasizes stages of processing, processing-capacity limitations, and the evolution of "strategies" or "heuristics" to simplify the spectator's task and bring it within capacity. Scientific research has explored the use of eye movement recording as a method of studying the role that the eyes play in analyzing and interpreting visual compositions. Pioneering work by Buswell [8] and Brandt [7] alludes to important differences in eye-fixation patterns between art-trained and untrained viewers, but these investigators were unable to quantify the nature of these differences. Similarly, by recording eye movements during the examination of a painting by Repin entitled "An Unexpected Visitor", the Russian scientist Yarbus [11] concluded that "composition is the means whereby the artist to some extent may compel the viewer to perceive what is portrayed in the picture." Unfortunately, Yarbus also failed to quantify differences in his viewer's scanpaths as he shifted the focus of visual attention by asking different questions about the meaning of the composition, leaving the burden of quantifying the relationship between eye fixations and compositional design to the reader's intuition.

Molnar has tried to quantify the role of eye fixation patterns in the evaluation of visual compositions [84, 85]. The mean duration of eye fixations for baroque art was about 60 msec briefer than for classical art. The general rule suggested by these data is that more complex pictures produce shorter eye fixations than less complex forms. This hypothesis has gained further support in [84] in which art experts were asked to judge the complexity of various types of art. Judgments were made of baroque pictures, classical paintings, and the art of Vasarely, Pollock, and Mondrian. A high degree of agreement was found among the experts as to what constituted complexity. Baroque paintings were judged to be more complex than classical paintings, and Pollock and Vasarely judged to be more complex than Mondrian. Eye fixations then follow the general rule stated above; complex pictures, such as baroque paintings, produce shorter fixation times than simple pictures. It may be that such complex art, which is densely packed with details, demands that attention be given to a large number of visual elements. This demand can be satisfied by allocating shorter fixation times to each feature. Simple figures, such as those created by many modern abstract artists, have far fewer features calling for attention, and therefore more time is allocated to each feature. Also, one could argue that in viewing abstract paintings, the viewer is trying to find a "deeper" meaning in each of the limited number of features – and thus spends more time on each [66].

Molnar assumes that eye fixations are driven either to seek knowledge or to seek pleasure. Exploration aimed at seeking knowledge is slower and more deliberate than that aimed at seeking pleasure. This has important implications for the quantification of spatial and temporal parameters of eye fixations. For example, Molnar has been able to differentiate "good" from "bad" compositions by recording the spatial density of fixations distributed over a painting during scanning.

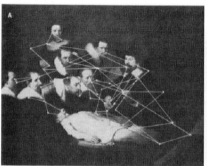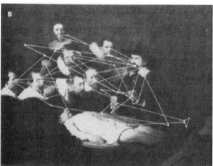

Figure 27. "Aesthetic" (early scanning, left) versus "Semantic" (late scanning, right) viewers' EM/Fixations of Rembrandt's "The anatomy lesson of Dr. Tulp", 1672 (from Molnar [84]).

Using graph theory, Molnar calculated the number of transitions or iterations in eye-fixation sequences from one area of a painting to another before a state of equilibrium is reached. Equilibrium reflects the end state of an ergodic process carried out by eye fixations in an attempt to grasp the aesthetic significance of the painting. It is the point at which the scanning pattern settles down on an average path after initially traversing a variable number of more-or-less random paths largely determined by pictorial features.

According to Molnar, the viewing of good compositions reaches equilibrium after fewer transitions than does the viewing of bad compositions, which he demonstrates by comparing transition-probability matrices from Manet's Olympia with Titian's Sacred Love. An important implication of this finding is that the aesthetic qualities of a visual composition are more likely to be sought during early scanning, presumably to satisfy diversive exploratory aims; late scanning is more likely to occur to satisfy cognitive curiosity, a specific exploration aim.

Evidence also suggests that different styles and periods of art produce different kinds of eye movements and fixations. Molnar pointed out the relationship between certain stylistic aspects of a picture and eye movements. Examples from the classical works of the high Renaissance were compared to examples from the mannerist and baroque periods that followed (which Molnar collectively labeled "baroque". Molnar found that classical art produces eye movements that are large and slow, reflecting the expansive nature of that style, while baroque paintings involve small and quick eye movements, reflecting the dense, animated character of that form.

i. The Role of Formal Art Training on Perception and Aesthetic Judgment of Art Compositions

The distinctions of eye fixation patterns were originally derived from theoretical notions about perception and attention that suggest that the visual information processing of pictures begins [81] at a global or preattentive level by segmenting the picture into figure and ground, and grasping the overall pattern variation, followed by a local-level analysis of interesting local pictorial features. The global-local distinction has proven useful in many tasks that involve the interpretation of pictures [66]. This distinction is useful in describing how viewers' eye fixations focus on pictorial features to isolate an embedded target object in a pictorial scene, e.g., finding the word "NINA" in Al Hirschfeld's drawings [71]. Reflecting different types of perceptual exploration, global exploration is pattern oriented, looking for the relationships in the layout of compositional elements, whereas local exploration is meaning oriented, focusing perception on the semantic properties of the individual elements that make up compositional themes. Locher and Nodine have found that widely dispersed fixations of short gaze duration (less than 300 msec) make up the majority of all fixations during initial viewing. As picture viewing proceeds, interspersed among these short gazes are increasing numbers of fixations of prolonged gaze duration (greater than 400 msec). The distributions of short and prolonged fixation durations during picture viewing suggest that short gazes carry out a global survey of the composition seeking out novel and interesting features. Prolonged gazes may intervene to resolve questions of meaning and significance to the overall compositional theme, carrying out a local survey. The results indicated that initially, subjects tend to exhibit widely dispersed fixations of short duration (less than 300 msec), suggesting a type of global viewing of the artwork indicative of diversive exploration. As viewing continues, however, there is a significant increase in the number of longer fixations (greater than 400 msec), which suggests a shift to more specific local, information-gathering activity. Aesthetic evaluation is of course based on both types of exploration. The eye-movement data of art-trained versus untrained viewers were examined by Nodine [71] to determine (1) if altering the balance of the original composition affected the way the viewer looked at the painting as revealed by the distributions of short- and long- duration gazes, which reflect differences in diversive and specific exploration; and (2) what design areas received the greatest visual attention by the viewer during perceptual analysis and judgment, which reflects differences in information-processing strategies.

They start with a citation of the general opinion that "is widely held among artists and teachers of art that the eyes can be trained to seek out aesthetic qualities of visual compositions and that this aspect of formal art training can directly influence a trained viewer's perceptual analysis and appreciation of visual compositions." This view rests mainly at the level of speculation, with little theoretical or empirical backing. One example of this position is taken from the late Richard Jung: "In general, the significance and beauty of art are only apparent to those who can see and are trained in viewing (Ibid.)", and ask then: "How does formal art training influence perception? i) Does such art training result in changes in how visual compositions are scanned and what type of information is processed during perceptual analysis? ii) How does the scanned information contribute to the formation of aesthetic judgments?" To answer these questions, they compared visual exploration patterns of art-trained and untrained viewers who judged compositions that differed in balance through manipulation of symmetrical organization. To answer their first question, eye-fixation patterns of art-trained and untrained groups were compared by measuring the amount of area coverage in 12 sec by diversive exploration – fixation durations of less than 300msec – and by specific exploration – fixation durations with longer than 400msec. To answer the second question, the eye fixation patterns were related to the type of pictorial information, based on the area analysis, processed by diversive and specific exploration defined by short- and long- gaze durations, respectively. They hypothesized that art-trained viewers would spend relatively more time overall engaged in diversive exploration than in specific exploration, since the viewing task focused attention on analysis of overall compositional design, not on individual pictorial elements. Each judgment consisted of a comparison between a formally balanced composition and its less formally balanced counterpart. Because the elements of a balanced composition correspond to a basic structure, their organization should facilitate the encoding component of visual information processing. The manipulation of compositional design consisted of removing, shifting or adding compositional elements to create a more or less balanced alternative. This was confirmed by the observation that artists intentionally spend more long-to-short gazes (specific to diversive exploration) for the less formal - less predictable – than the more formal – more predictable – compositional designs, while untrained viewers reiterated the inverse patterns. This was similar to results of [66]. They showed a difference between the eye movements of art-trained viewers and those of untrained viewers under these conditions. Trained viewers spent relatively more time in diversive exploration than in specific exploration when viewing the altered pictures, while untrained viewers performed just the opposite. Subjects who had had extensive art training tended to concentrate on finding thematic patterns among compositional elements, while the untrained subjects tended to concentrate on representational and semantic use of picture elements. Nodine concluded that "untrained viewers failed to recognize the perceptual organizing functions of symmetry, focusing attention instead on the representational issue of how accurately individual elements conveyed 'objective' reality." Art training seems to teach viewers to appreciate paintings not because, in Levi-Strauss's words, "they are good to see," but because they are "good to think". This suggests that beauty is less in the eye, and more in the mind of the beholder. This insightful analysis fits well with our general idea and manyfold explications given here. It is also well attuned to current theories in visual perception stressing the cognitive basis of art. We "think" art as much as, or even more, that we "see" art [86]. These studies by Nodine therefore support Berlyne's notion that aesthetic preferences are based on both types of exploration.

Art through art?

Erwin Panofsky said in his essay "About the Problem of Style in Creative Art": "Can we say that it is only the eye whose changed perspective brings out now a pictorial, now a linear, now a subordinating, now a coordinating style? And if we could agree to put it that way, i.e., to call the potential of the linear, etc., visual options, and to call that which determines the choice of one or the other special behavioural options of the eye – would we be entitled to see in the eye and its movements a wholly organic, totally apsychological instrument, one whose relation to the world is principally distinct from that of the soul to the world?" Panofsky's question indicated the point at which his critique of Wölfflin's teaching set in. The concepts of "seeing", the "eye", the "visual" have no absolutely clear meaning. The individual sciences use them in two distinct senses, which must be clearly distinguished in a methodological investigation: one literal, and one metaphorical. In its strictly literal meaning, the eye is an organ which in the first place gives to man a merely subjectively felt "reality", thence by relating that which is perceived to an aprioristic notion of abstract space, a "reality" made objective. The perception of the latter may be called a visual experience, or "seeing". Basing one's reasoning on this physiological-objective concept of seeing, one would indeed be fully justified in considering seeing as appertaining to an "inferior" sphere of artistic activity, this side of anything expressive. It has thus nothing to do with emotion or temperament, for if the visual impression of one person is different from that of another; "this is due only to myopia, hyperopia, astigmatism, or impaired color perception. A person taking that view would have to admit, though, that seeing in this sense plays no role whatsoever in developing a style. The eye as an organ, which can recognize but not create forms, knows nothing of what is "pictorial" or "areal", of "closed" or "open" forms. "Seeing" in its non-metaphorical sense is this side of any expression, but also this side of what Wölfflin calls Optik." In this respect, André Malraux's principle, "art through art", remains of paramount importance. The lawfulness of art, as embodied in representative groups of paintings, is his concern. The art historian Bearden (1976) insists on the "Malraux principle" and appears not to be interested in the viewer's model – unless he/she is an artist. He prefers to point to the relation between models of artists of different kind and times – which is why he also likes to refer to the postmodernistic era. Though the painter's mind is infinitely varied and will be inspired, will flourish, and will nurture under a host of differing stimuli and actions, it is obvious that Malraux's principle, "art through art," has survived and even has been confirmed repeatedly during the last decades of art production in the "post-modernistic era". Naturally, the painter's mind (where his model is located) is most truly be reflected (translated) in the works he has created. Space in this context means: The painter's realization of space – Space and the historical movement – Space Movement and countermovement – Spatial Relations. Space, order and science represent therefore the "golden section". About the object, space and the collective consciousness the artist may be able to tap, W. Haftmann (1953) reflects in the early 1950ies:

"To the painter who confronts the outer world, the latter appears to him as an object in space: object and space are his two basic constants. But both have moved into a changed dimension with modern painting. Where modern painting approaches things directly and seeks to describe itself in terms of the greatest detachment, there is still some hint of that "different" reality". He states that out of this modern experience of things is born the specific variety of modern realism, which we call "magic realism"

(Carrà) or "transcendent realism" (Beckmann). In order to take this experience of things to its ultimate limit, provocative and experimental techniques have been sought out within modern painting by the Dadaist and surrealist movements. In doing so, they aim at taking things out of their ordinary frames of reference and through the shock caused by confrontation with the absurdity of their appearance in their new frames of reference showing up the hidden ambiguity of things:

"Their "Phantastik in härtester Materie" (fantastic nature in the hardest matter). The object thus enters into a relationship with that unknown, magic interactant" (Werner Haftmann "About Modern Painting" 1953).

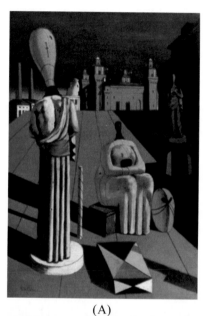

(A)

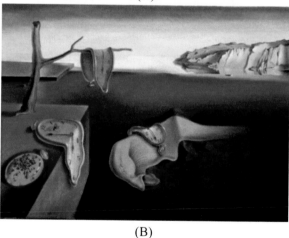

(B)

Figure 28. The specific variety of modern realism, which we call "magic realism" (Chirico, up, "The disturbing muses" 1918) or "sur-realism" (Dali, bottom, "The persistence of Memory", 1931).

3. NOTES ON VISUAL PERCEPTION

To the normal observer objects in the world not only appear organized but they appear organized in particular ways. One way is hierarchically. There are objects that are distinct yet embedded within other objects. A room might contain desks, filing cabinets, and desk drawers, but the desk contains desk drawers and not rooms or filing cabinets. Given this kind of perceived organization, it is reasonable to suspect that there are mechanisms that operate to connect objects hierarchically. Hierarchical scenes in which some distinct objects are embedded within other objects occur in many situations. A common illustration is a face that, as a compound figure, is composed of eyes, a nose, and a mouth, etc. The latter are embedded in the face and they can also be recognized as distinct objects. What is the order of processing when we see these kinds of compound patterns? Is the whole perceived first and then decomposed into parts, or conversely, are parts perceived first and then integrated into a unified whole? Relative hemispheric specialization for global and local processing as found in other neuropsychological studies appears to prevail. In the directed attention task, subjects were required to attend to either the global or local level of the stimuli throughout all trials, attention to global aspect resulted in significant activation of the right lingual gyrus; when attention focused on local aspects the left inferior occipital cortex was activated. Contextual conditions are varied by different pairings of scenes with target objects. More than 40 years ago, Steven Palmer [19] performed an experiment that demonstrated the influence of the prior presentation of visual scenes on the identification of briefly presented drawings of real-world objects, used different pairings of objects and scenes to produce three main contextual conditions: appropriate, inappropriate, and no context. Neurological patients with damage to either the parietal or temporal visual areas show deficits on attention and visual search tasks and the pattern of deficits points to specific roles for the different areas. Understanding visual imagery can help to explain these deficits. The important question is, to specify what an image is: Do images rely, at least in part, on depictive representations, or are the depictive aspects evident to introspection merely concomitants of propositional processing?

Kosslyn has shown that objects in images are inspected using the same mechanisms that are used to encode and interpret objects during perception [51]. That previously learned skills or talents can be conserved in the setting of dementia has been described for some time. Demented individuals have been reported who maintained musical skills, painting talents, and word game skills. Especially remarkable is the businessman who became an artist in the setting of dementia and whose paintings steadily improved despite progressive cognitive decline. At 58 years he became anomic and disinhibited. Language and memory deteriorated, but he showed heightened visual and auditory awareness. In a recent discussion of the unexpected occurrence of behavioral improvement following brain injury, the term "**paradoxical functional facilitation**" was used. Whereas in normal subjects, inhibitory and excitatory mechanisms interact in a complex harmony, the role of inhibitory processes may be critical in mediating specific restorative paradoxical functional facilitation effects. It is well accepted that talent in one area, such as art, may be accompanied by dysfunction in other spheres, such as social skills. The loss of social skills and inhibitions may have facilitated the art of the described patient.

a. Selective Visual Attention

Recent developments of positron emitting tomography (PET) and functional magnetic resonance imaging (fMRI) studies have shown a large number of focal interdependencies between primary and higher visual "centers" besides the "what" and "where" paths. Additional studies using repetitive transcranial magnetic stimulation (rTMS) have demonstrated transient functional lesions, concerning the vision of movement, color and also synaesthetic perceptions of kinaesthetic, visual and vestibular content.

Focusing of our attention to a sensory modality enhances the cerebral metabolism in the corresponding primary sensory cortex. It may be asked then whether focusing of vision to a selective feature of a visual stimulus may also raise the regional cerebral blood flow (rCBF) in those cortical areas specifically engaged for processing this information. Selective visual attention highlights certain areas that are located in the network of visual cortical areas. In activation tasks exploring selective visual attention Corbetta et al. [87] demonstrated that attention to *speed* activated a region in the left inferior parietal lobule, attention to *color* a region in the dorsolateral occipital cortex, and attention to *shape* activated the collateral sulcus and the temporal cortex along the superior temporal sulcus. It was demonstrated that the activity in extrastriate V4 reflected selection that was based on the cued feature and not simply on the physical color. These experiments on selection of visual cues across the entire receptive fields of extrastriate V4 neurons provided an alternative to earlier finding by Moran and Desimone [88] who demonstrated a spatial restriction of focal attentive processes across the entire receptive field of V4. Functional MRI measurements showed that attention-driven cortical activity precisely matched the topography of activity evoked by the cued targets when presented in isolation [89]. Specifically, such a retinotopic mapping of attention-related activation was found in primary visual cortex, as well as in dorsomedial and ventral occipital visual areas previously implicated in processing the attended target features. The activation of visual association areas was not restricted to purely perceptive visual tasks but could also be demonstrated in visuomotor performance tasks.

b. Visual Perception Damage

Injury to the brain like a stroke can severely impair our ability to attend to parts of our visual world despite normal visual acuity. Self-portraits were made by the German artist Anton Raederscheidt in the months following a stroke that damaged the right parietal lobe with the consequence of visual neglect. At first he quite remarkably omitted half the face (Figure 29, upper left), but had gradually recovered his ability by the end of nine months (upper right, lower left and finally lower right).

Figure 29. Injury to the brain like a stroke can severely impair our ability to attend to parts of our visual world despite normal visual acuity. These self-portraits were made by the German artist Anton Raederscheidt in the months following a stroke that damaged the right parietal lobe with the consequence of visual neglect. At first, he quite remarkably omitted half the face (upper left), but had gradually recovered his ability by the end of nine months (upper right, lower left and finally lower right).

Significant metabolic depressions occur contralateral to the hemineglect in premotor and parietal, peri-insular, and cingulate cortex, and subcortically in the thalamus, the sensorimotor cortex around the central sulcus is spared. Visual perception is severely disturbed after damage to the visual cortical areas. Destruction of the primary visual cortex inducing cortical blindness is most often caused by cerebrovascular disease and sometimes accompanied by denial of blindness by the patients [90]. In chronic lesions of one occipital lobe some patients can respond to visual stimuli presented within their contralateral clinically blind visual hemifield. Since in this situation the visual motion area became activated without concurrent activation of the primary visual cortex, segregated thalamocortical projections to different parts of the extrastriate cortex were good, but not exclusive candidates for providing the anatomic basis for this residual function [91]. Evidence from lesion studies in primates showed that the cortical area adjacent to the primary visual cortex played an important role for the discrimination of complex spatial stimuli, but did not affect the discrimination of low-level visual information such as color or size [92]. Psychophysical experiments in monkeys showed that the time course of visual perception paralleled the increase of neuronal activity upon complex visual stimulation [93]. Conversely, magnetic stimulation of the occipital cortex in humans was reported to interfere with visual perception and visual short-term memory [94]. Further evidence for the paramount role of the extrastriate cortex for the perception of complex visual stimuli could be derived from a patient with hypoxemic cortical blindness. This patient developed visual hallucinations during recovery of vision accompanied by normalization of cortical function in extrastriate cortex as revealed by positron emitting tomograpy (PET) imaging [95]. During the hallucinations regional cerebral blood flow (rCBF) increases not only occurred in the left and right *occipital gyri* but also in the right *temporal* and *parietal,* and left frontal gyrus, suggesting activation of a large-scale network for her vivid visual perceptions [95].

c. Neuropsychological Findings Relevant for Neurology of Perception

To the normal observer objects in the world not only appear organized but they appear organized in particular ways. One way is hierarchically, where objects are distinct yet embedded within other objects: A room might contain desks, filing cabinets, and desk drawers, but the desk contains desk drawers and not rooms or filing cabinets. Given this kind of perceived organization, it is reasonable to suspect that there are mechanisms that operate to connect objects hierarchically.

Both normal and neuropsychological evidence also suggests that a modular system is responsible for the organization of parts and wholes by the visual system and there is a hierarchical organization of objects within objects that involves the coordination of at least *four separate subsystems: one* that emphasizes the global properties of a figure (right temporal-parietal regions), *one* that emphasizes the local properties of a figure (left temporal-parietal regions), *one* that controls the distribution of attentional resources to these subsystems (right or left lateral parietal region), and *one* that interconnects global and local properties (posterior temporal-temporal pathways).

On seeing with the pictorially viewing eye that perceives a "communion of objects"

At the turn of the 20[th]century the art historian H. Wölfflin tried to express the development of art by pairs of concepts: The development from the linear to the pictorial, that is the development of the line as a viewing aid and a guide for the eye, and the successive devaluation of the line:

"More generally speaking: the comprehension of bodies in their tactile nature – as contours and areas – on the one hand –, and on the other, an attitude that is capable of renouncing itself to the mere visual appearance and doing without the palpable drawing. The one stresses the limitation of things, in the other the appearance touches on the limitless. Seeing forms and contours isolates the objects, while the pictorially viewing eye perceives a communion of objects."

In this respect, John Berger noted on viewing art:

"Images were first made to conjure up the appearances of something that was absent. Gradually it became evident that an image could outlast what it represented; it then showed how something or somebody had looked in the past. Touch may be described as a static, limited form of sight, showing only limited relation to past experience. Our vision is continually active, continually moving, continually holding things in a circle around itself, constituting what is present to us as we are. We never look at just one thing; we are always looking at the relation between things and ourselves, so we can remember them."

In these observations and statements Berger seems to be relatively close to some of the comments of the presocratic philosophers on visual perception twentysixhundred years ago: Reciprocity of vision and its bottom-upness are seen and described as related facts.

With respect to Bonnard (Figure 30) John Elderfield [96] stresses the low level bottom up details of his paintings as put forward by the artist himself:

"Bonnard famously observed that painting was "the transcription of the adventures of the optic nerve", but criticism has been slow to acknowledge why a painting by Bonnard might usefully be thought of not as a representation of substance but as a representation of the perception of substance."

In 1962 David Sylvester wondered whether Bonnard was re-creating the process of seeing, noticing how looking at his paintings seemed, effectively, to reproduce both the sensation of loss of acuity at the periphery of the visual field and the creation of a scanpath of eye movements between focal points, fixated for varying durations and, consequently, with varying attentive interest. Bonnard replaced "artificial perspective" by the record of "*natural vision*":

"Because the eye, wherever it is directed in a painting by Bonnard, meets patches too large to be within the resolving power of foveal vision, there is nowhere for the fovea to pick up fine detail. But as the fovea moves away from an array of patches, they will form into continuous colors and edges, swing to the lower resolving power of parafoveal and peripheral vision. The pictorial field of a Bonnard, then, may be thought to resent not "natural vision", decreasing in acuity from fovea to periphery, but the very obverse of that, an increase in acuity from fovea to periphery" [97].

What Bonnard calls the variability of vision is accompanied by what he calls its mobility. Vision is mobile, in so far as the viewing eye constantly, restlessly changes its direction so as to redirect its acuity within the visual field to cause an image to fall onto the fovea, the retina's tiny central area of maximum acuity under conditions of bright illumination:

"These conjunctive eye movements may either be smooth, when the eye is turned willfully according to the demands of attention, or saccadic, when the eye turns "in fixation reflexes" that may respond to the stimuli of parafoveal and peripheral information" [98].

It is important to add, that the direction of central, foveal vision by cognitive demands for information about objects can be overridden by the more quickly and automatically operating system stimulated by parafoveal and peripheral vision. This has a crucial bearing on the painter's attentional direction and the beholder's temporal experience of a painting.

Figure 30. Bonnard: "Landscape" 1922. Clockwise sequence of fixations during 3 sec; note the change of fixations from background [out of window] towards right foreground [undefined subject's head reclining on a couch], – there is nowhere for the fovea to pick up detail [70].

d. Different Psychophysiological Processing of Wholes and Parts

Hierarchical scenes in which some distinct objects are embedded within other objects occur in many situations. A common illustration is a face that, as a compound figure, is composed of eyes, a nose, and a mouth, etc. The latter are embedded in the face and they can also be recognized as distinct objects. What is the order of processing when we see these kinds of compound patterns? Is the whole perceived first and then decomposed into parts, or conversely, are parts perceived first and then integrated into a unified whole? Concerning the relation between wholes and constituent parts of a stimulus, structuralism holds that the perception of a whole object can be analyzed into its constituent parts, and the basic units of perception are independent local sensations. The perceived whole is nothing more than the sum of its perceived parts (Figure 31). Most models of human vision are based on this view, i.e., the analysis of a pattern's independent parts and their features is usually assigned to the first stage of processing [79, 99]. In contrast, gestalt psychologists claimed that the whole is different from the sum of its parts. They stressed the function of perceptual organization, suggesting that the dominance of wholes, which results from basic organizational principles such as proximity and similarity, determines whether the wholes or parts are recognized first (see first Chapter). The controversy between these two schools of thought still attracts interest since it is closely related to a central issue understanding vision: Where does visual information processing begin?

Among the approaches to the investigation of whole-part relation in the last two decades, Navon's paradigm, using compound stimulus patterns with small letters nested within a larger letter, played a major role (Figure 31). In this paradigm, the global aspect of a stimulus is formally identified with the properties of the large letters, and the local aspect is defined by the property of the small letters. The identity of the global and large letters can be the same (the consistent condition) or different (the inconsistent condition). Navon [100] found that subjects responded faster to the global letters than the local ones (i.e., there was a global advantage reaction time, or RT); and RTs for local letters were longer in the inconsistent condition than in the content condition (i.e., there was global interference at the local level), but the identity of the local letters did not affect RT for global letters (i.e., there was no interference). On the basis of these results, Navon advanced the global precedence hypotheses, which stated that visual pattern processing proceeds from a global level to a more local level. His global precedence hypothesis assumes that the processing of the global level of a hierarchical pattern precedes that of the local level. The event-related brain Potentials (ERPs) associated with identifying the global and local levels of nonlinguistic compound stimuli in a selective attention task shed some light on this hypothesis: While subjects' behavioral responses were similar to those observed by Navon, the analyses of ERP data showed that identification of the local level elicited longer and decreased identification of the global level.

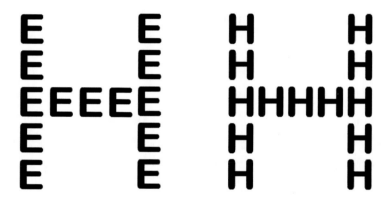

Figure 31. Large letters made out of small letters to test the whole-part relation.

e. Global/Local Visual Processing

The right hemisphere is dominant for many visuospatial functions, although recent neuropsychological experiments suggest that the pattern of hemispheric asymmetry is more complex than a simple dichotomy: each hemisphere is dominant to processing different types of visual information [101]. Psychological studies using stimuli with larger figures [global forms made of smaller figures, i.e., local components] show global precedence [100].

The functional anatomy involved in sustaining or switching visual attention between different perceptual levels, using functional imaging measures of neural activity was recently studied. Two experiments were carried out using hierarchically organized letters, i.e., large letters made out of small letters. In a divided-attention task, subjects were required to switch attention between local and global levels. The number of successive stimuli for which subjects had to sustain attention to either the global or local level co-varied significantly, with temporal-parietal activations bilaterally. The number of switches between levels co-varied significantly with activations in the left supplementary motor area and the left medial parietal cortex. Relative hemispheric specialization for global and local processing as found in other neuropsychological studies appears to prevail. In the directed attention task, subjects were required to attend to either the global or local level of the stimuli throughout all trials, attention to global aspect resulted in significant activation of the right lingual gyrus; when attention focused on local aspects the left inferior occipital cortex was activated.

Viewing pictures with insufficient magnification and poor visual resolution can be compared between experts and non-experts. Non-experts may show an insufficient cognitive skill, e.g., when viewing highly artistic pictures of realistic content (e.g., P. Brueghel), or of completely abstract content (e.g., M. Rothko). Virtual examples, i.e., a fish and a pair of shoes are shown with the assumption that a similar control mechanism holds for eye movements in picture viewing and reading [102]. Visual information processing with insufficient stimulus size may be found in small print of telephone books or in footnotes. Examples of insufficient object sizes in picture viewing are also found in paintings containing few large and many small objects i.e., landscapes and groups of subjects as in paintings by Brueghel or Canaletto. Viewers tend to overcome the resulting visibility problems by reducing the viewing distance. In museums one observes the common practice to view such paintings from a far and a close distance. Magnifications below the optimal skill-matching values require additional processing time for safely recognizing the details: This causes the number and duration of local fixations to increase. The index "g/l" is the ratio of global/local saccades that is in non-experts much smaller than in experts. Global saccades are of 5deg-10 deg, local saccades are of 1 deg to 4 deg. Magnifications below the skill-matching level are associated with a decrease of eye movement speed.

Experts/adults show optimal performance with object/letter sizes matching visual acuity and cognitive skill according to the size ability matching condition. Each of several (e.g., four) objects or words are processed with one fixation rendering a total processing time of about 1 sec. The picture viewing global/local (g/l) index is 0.75, given by 3 large saccades between the four objects. This renders a mean eye movement speed of about 10 deg/s in reading. The processing problems of non-experts/children in second grade when they have to use the same size of objects or letters as experts/adults are as follows: With the normal cognitive processing ability in second grade of about 0.2, skill-matching letter sizes of less than half the normal reading speed should result. Since letters of normal size are only about half the skill-matching size defined by the size ability matching condition, fixation duration increases by about 20%.

The intermittent mode of data acquisition in visual information processing is unique in sensory physiology and consists of data acquisition periods of about 250 ms when the eye is stationary (sampled data model [103]). These time periods are required because of the slow photochemical reactions in the receptor cells which encode visual information. Cognitive skills, like a software, serve to make optimal use of the retina, as a hardware, and a working memory allows the smooth transformation of the collected stationary retinal images into a continuous flow of language or picture context. Under optimal reading conditions, the 2 deg retinal fovea is moved in a step-like manner 4 times per second resulting in a mean eye movement speed of about 8 deg/s. In picture viewing the eye movement speed depends on the number, difficulty, and spacing of objects. Optimal processing conditions are reached in picture viewing (and reading) when the image magnification is inversely proportional to visual acuity or cognitive skill. This ensures rapid letter/object recognition by the high resolution of the central retina. Letters or objects too small to be processed visually or cognitively during the optimal sampling intervals cause a processing overload: Fixations become more closely spaced and have longer than normal durations. In addition, eye movement speed falls below the optimal value of 8 deg/s; in picture viewing the g/l index of global (large) to local (small) saccades decreases together with the eye movement speed. Letters or objects that are too large lead to higher than normal eye movement speed, which is equally non-optimal for recognition. Because cognitive skill controls top down eye movements in picture viewing and reading, a similar magnification may be appropriate for both types of visual information processing, picture viewing and reading.

f. Effects of Contextual Scenes on Identification

Contextual conditions are varied by different pairings of scenes with target objects. More than 40 years ago, Steven Palmer [19] performed an experiment that demonstrated the influence of the prior presentation of visual scenes on the identification of briefly presented drawings of real-world objects, used different pairings of objects and scenes to produce three main contextual conditions: appropriate, inappropriate, and no context. Correct responses and confusions with visually similar objects depended strongly on both the contextual condition and the particular target object presented. The probability of being correct was highest in the appropriate context condition and lowest in the inappropriate context condition. Confidence ratings of responses were a function of the perceptual similarity between the stimulus object and the named object; they were not strongly affected by contextual conditions. Many theories of perception stress this interaction of sensory input. While psychologists differ in their formulations of how context affects perception, they agree that appropriate context should aid identification and that inappropriate context should hinder it. This general result has been established in the recognition of words using sentences as contexts and in the recognition of letters using words as contexts. Related effects are present in visual search phenomena: Less time is required to find a target object within an appropriate scene than within an inappropriate scene. Palmer's experiment [19] demonstrated the importance of contextual scenes for object identification in terms of correct responses and confusions with visually similar stimuli.

g. Cognitive Channels Computing Action Distance and Direction

Visually guided, goal-directed reaching requires encoding of action distance and direction from attributes of visual landmarks. A cognitive mechanism that seemingly performs visual motor extension before action initiation has been identified. These extended earlier findings concerning a mechanism for visual motor mental rotation. Humans systematically delay action onset while newly planning increasingly distant arm movements beyond a visual landmark, consistent with an internal representation for visual motor extension. Onset times also change systematically during concurrent mental rotation and visual motor extension computations required to process new directions and distances. Visual motor extension associated with reaching is slowed down when participants need to plan action direction within the same time frame, whereas mental rotation efficiency stays unaffected by concurrent needs to prepare action distance. In contrast to parallel direction and distance computations needed for direct aiming to a visual target, the planning of new directions and distances likely occurs at distinct times.

h. Temporal Aspects of Visual Search Studied by Transcranial Magnetic Stimulation (TMS)

Neurological patients with damage to either the parietal or temporal visual areas show deficits on attention and visual search tasks and the pattern of deficits points to specific roles for the different areas. Lesions that include parts of the occipito-parietal cortex can impair serial conjunction searches, but not parallel, "pop-out" searches. Damage to the occipito-temporal visual areas can impair some parallel visual search tasks, but not serial, conjunction search [104]. The distinction between parallel and serial visual search provides a heuristic for analyzing the processes involved in detecting a target stimulus in a complex visual array. Search tasks may parse some of the components involved in suprathreshold vision by varying the frequency with which stimuli appear, the complexity of the targets, the familiarity of the targets and distractors. The richness of visual search tasks allows also to ask questions about the integration of processing between the so-called dorsal and ventral visual occipito-parieto-temporal processing streams. Selective spatial attention, memory for the target, object-based attention over large areas of the visual field and identification of the target are all required in visual search, and these components are commonly associated with dorsal-parietal (spatial attention) and ventral-temporal stream (memory and identification) visual areas. Transcranial magnetic stimulation (TMS) can be used to simulate the effects of highly circumscribed brain damage permanently present in some neuropsychological patients, by reversibly disrupting the normal functioning of the cortical area to which it is applied. Transcranial magnetic stimulation over the parietal visual cortex of subjects while they were performing "popout" or conjunction visual search tasks in arravs containing eight distractors has no detrimental effect on the performance of pop-out search. But it does significantly increase reaction times on conjunction search. Stimulation has no effect on the number of errors made. This suggests that a sub-region of the right parietal lobe is important for conjunction search but not for preattentive pop-out. They are consistent with timing data from studies of single cells in monkeys and the hypothesis that parietal areas generate a signal that projects back to extrastriate visual areas to enhance the processing of features in a restricted part of the visual field. The timing of the effect indicates that transcranial stimulation disrupts the mechanisms underlying the focal attention necessary for feature binding in conjunction search.

i. Disorder of Visual Attention in Parkinson's Disease

Selective attention is the gateway to conscious experience, affecting our ability to perceive, distinguish and remember the various stimuli that come our way; it denotes the allocation of limited processing resources to some stimuli or tasks at the expense of others. Besides its effects on perception or memory, selective attention is a significant contributor to *motor control,* determining which of the various objects in the visual field is to be the target used *to plan and guide movement.*

As selective visual attention allows us to concentrate on one aspect of the visual field while ignoring other things, it is modulated by both, involuntarily bottom-up and voluntary top down mechanisms within a brainstem-parietotemporal and basal-ganglia-frontal neuronal network [105, 3]. Frontal executive deficits are typical in Parkinson's disease (PD) [106] and activity of basal ganglia-frontal motor areas is altered in PD patients in symptomatic [107] even presymptomatic [108] stages. This results in impairment of the response selection system in PD, which leads to an inability to remove inhibition from an intended program and an inability to inhibit competing programs [109].

Results of visual attentions tasks depend on accurate saccade programming that leads to an obligatory shift of attention to the saccade's target before the voluntary eye movement is executed. This is due to two parameters: correct programming of the saccade and correct saccade dynamics. Impairment of central, top down, programming deficits influence oculomotor function; and vice versa the resulting oculomotor dysfunction could have a direct, bottom up impact on results of visual attention tasks. Because selective visual attention for spatial locations is under control of the same neural circuits as those in charge of motor programming of saccades visual attention as well as ocular saccades are impaired in PD. In a conjoined feature search task of PD patients, saccadic oculomotor control and hand reaction times were intact, whereas visual selective attention and hand movement time was not. Successful searches were found in 30% of PD patients and in 40% of controls, i.e., PD patients did 25% worse in this test [108].

Chan et al. [110] showed PD patient's inability to plan eye movements to remembered target locations, suggesting that they have a deficit in spatial working memory and time-sequencing along with their deficit in automatic saccade suppression, which is consistent with a disorder of the prefrontal-basal-ganglia circuit. Impairment of this pathway could release the automatic saccade system from top down inhibition and produce deficits in volitional saccade control. In scanpath memory-guided saccades

– as in visual imagery paradigms – movement memory improves the accuracy of memory-guided saccades [111]. Maioli et al. [112] examined timing and scanpaths of eye movements during a visual search task, in which subjects had to detect as quickly as possible the presence or absence of a target among distractors. Data show that this task was characterized by quantitative rather than by qualitative differences in search strategy: The number of saccades made during search predicted very accurately the *time* required to accomplish the task; fixation times were independent of the number of stimulus items. In addition, when PD patients scan pictures, they explore a smaller area of them with smaller saccades compared to normal subjects.

j. Motion-Blindness Induced by Magnetic Stimulation of Human Visual Area V5

The region (V5) of the human visual cortex, which lies in the occipital lobe posterior to the junction of the inferior temporal and lateral occipital sulci, is specialized for the analysis of visual motion. Brain imaging studies report an increase in activation in and around area V5 when subjects have deficits in perceiving motion which range from an almost total inability to perceive the movement of objects to deficits in second-order motion only. In an attempt to recreate deficits similar to those reported in motion-blind patients and to assess the specificity of deficits when TMS is applied over human areaV5, the (extrastriate) parieto-occipital area for motion-sensitivity, visual search tasks have been used [94]. These studies show that subjects are impaired in a motion but not a form of "pop-out'" task when TMS is applied over V5. When motion is present, but irrelevant, or when attention to colour and form were required, TMS applied to V5 enhances performance. When attention to motion is required in a motion-form conjunction search task, irrespective of whether the target is moving or stationary, TMS disrupts performance. This shows that attention to different visual attributes involves mutual inhibition between different extrastriate visual areas.

k. Concerning Explanations of Imagery

Concerning explanations of imagery there are two central issues. One is to specify what an image is: Do images rely, at least in part, on depictive representations, or are the depictive aspects evident to introspection merely concomitants of propositional processing? Given that the size of an imaged object shifts the pattern of activity in at least one occipital visual area (identified as area 17), there is good evidence that image representations are depictive. This is corroborated by studies in brain damaged patients. Farah et al. [113] reported that a patient who had an occipital lobe resection in one hemisphere was only able to image objects over about half the horizontal visual angle that the patient could prior to the surgery. The second issue concerns the question, what "looks" at patterns of imageries, and how are images generated and transformed?

There is a lot of evidence that imagery and perception share common mechanisms. Convergent evidence from PET and repetitive TMS (rTMS) concerning the role of area 17 in visual imagery has been reported by Kosslyn et al. [114]. The rTMS results showed an impairment of the information processing of area 17, and the PET results showed that when patterns of stripes are visualized, area 17 is activated. The results from PET studies support the notion of decomposition of high level visual processing, and have demonstrated that imagery does indeed rely on many of the same mechanisms used in top down hypothesis testing during perception. The mechanisms underlying imagery seem similar to those underlying visual perception – which is not surprising, since many of the same mechanisms underlie both abilities. Kosslyn has shown that objects in images are inspected using the same mechanisms that are used to encode and interpret objects during perception. When we seek a specific object, part, or characteristic, its "representation in the pattern activation" subsystems of EM are primed; if the object, part, or characteristic is depicted in the image, it will "pop out" if its representation is activated in the pattern activation subsystem. Through image inspection information in memory can be accessed when the sought information is not represented propositionally and cannot be deduced. Also, when the image generation and inspection process is faster than the process of retrieving and using propositional information. Scanning is accomplished by shifting the attention window and by image transformation. People can perform transformations such as rotating, translating, scaling, bending, or folding objects, and reinterpret the transformed shape, unless representations that preserve the local geometry of the object are modified: This claim is consistent with the finding that the occipital lobe is activated during image rotation [115]. Functional MRI data [116] suggests increased activity in area Vl when people rotate Shepard and Metzler figures. Visual mental images may be transformed in part via motor processes [51]. This hypothesis first occurred to him when he saw a brain-damaged patient behaving oddly in a mental rotation task: When the stimulus appeared on the screen, the patient consistently reached up to the screen and pretended to twist the stimulus. "Image transformations are not accomplished by a single process. Motion encoded transformations occur when one activates a representation of an object that was encoded while it was moving, which produces a moving image. Motion-added transformations occur when an imaged object is made to move in a novel way." During perception, the shape shift subsystem systematically alters representations in the spatiotopic mapping subsystem and alters the imagery mapping function. At the same time, the pattern activation subsystems are activated helping to encode the expected consequences of performing a specific action. During imagery, this causes an image to form. As the spatial representations are altered, also the mapping functions are altered to be consistent with the new spatial properties. "The resulting image transformations are continuous if the anticipated perceptual input is continuous" [51].

l. Kosslyn's Principle of Visual Perception

The shape shift subsystem may receive input from motor programming subsystems – but it also receives input from more complex processes that allow one to predict how events will unfold. Thus, it allows us to visualize what we expect to see when manipulating an object, it also permits to visualize what we would expect to see when objects interact – the key is that one anticipates what one would see if a specific sequence occurred. This process of predicting the sequence of events involves stored knowledge. "One can transform either the entire field, e.g., by anticipating what one would see as one turned one's head in a room, or a selected object, part, or characteristic – by surrounding it with the attention window and altering the mapping function to that object or part. In some circumstances one can transform objects by allowing one image to fade and generating a new one that is altered in the specified way" [51]. There are two type of image transformations: one is a "replay" of a stored transformation: such objects changed over time when viewed, and the subsequent mental image also changes over time. The other type consists of transforming an object in a novel way. Novel transformations rely on a shape shift subsystem – according to Kosslyn, "which alters the representation of an object's spatial properties and alters the imagery mapping function while the pattern activation subsystems are primed to encode a sequence of stimuli." This prepares a viewer's perception to encode what he would see while performing an action or watching some other action. In imagery, the viewer visualizes what he would expect to see if some object were manipulated or in some other way handled. If image transformations are evoked by motor processes, and the brain is wired so that one anticipates what one will see as one moves, then the brain will respect the laws of physics that govern movements, and images will be transformed continuously. Since objects are constrained to move along trajectories, if the viewer anticipates how some action will unfold, this too will result in a continuously changing image. During perception, one can attend to an entire shape. It can be stored as a particular example or as a

member of a shape category, which representations later may be activated to form an image of a single global shape. A pattern code in associative memory that is associated with that object is sent "downstream" to specify a prototype or a specific example, which will correspond best to a representation. Hints about why imagery "feels" the way it does, are given if image transformations depend in part on motor processing, e.g., why people sometimes feel as if they are physically manipulating objects during imagery.

m. Example of Art Production with Neurological Deficits Occurring in the Course of Alzheimer's Disease

That previously learned skills or talents can be conserved in the setting of dementia has been described for some time. Demented individuals have been reported who maintained musical skills, painting talents, and word game skills. Especially remarkable is the businessman who became an artist in the setting of dementia [117, 118] and whose paintings steadily improved despite progressive cognitive decline.

"A 68- ear-old right-handed man was seen for a dementing illness of a 12-year duration. Previously a successful businessman without interest in art, at age 56 he began to describe "open" and "closed" periods. When "closed", he was dysphoric, when "open" the experienced lights and sounds produced a pleasant feeling that allowed him to think creatively. He painted images experienced during "open" and "closed" periods. At 58 years he became anomic and disinhibited. Language and memory deteriorated, but he showed heightened visual and auditory awareness. Odd compulsions developed, and despite his considerable wealth, he convinced his caregivers to walk with him to look for coins. At the age of 56 he began painting. During the next decade he created paintings with increasing precision and detail. The first featured brightly colored ellipses. Soon his work became realistic, and he drew animals. Later works were crafted with care, and he took hours to complete single lines. Between 63 and 66 years his paintings won several art show awards. By age 68 he drew oddly shaped doll-like figures. On examination he was remote and irritable, showing little facial emotion. He displayed heightened interest in his environment, commenting extensively on color and sound. His MiniMentalScore was 15, and his verbal output was fluent. A mild comprehension deficit and a semantic anomia were present"

The MRI showed bitemporal atrophy worse on the left than the right, and PET revealed bilateral temporal hypoperfusion (worse on the right than the left). Frontal perfusion was normal. Regions with highest perfusion were the right primary visual cortex and the right posterior parietal lobe.

In view of these findings, the artistic products of patients like the one described are diverse but share many features. The creativity is visual but never verbal: The paintings, photographs, and sculptures created are mostly copies lacking an abstract or symbolic component. The paintings of these patients remind of realistic landscapes, animals, or people. The painters seemed to recall images that were then mentally reconstructed as pictures without the mediation of language. Also, despite progressive cognitive and social impairment, they showed increasing interest in the fine detail of faces, objects, shapes, and sounds. Also there is a preoccupation with art in many of these patients, and their search for perfection that enhances the quality of their art [119]. The anatomic substrate for these patients may indicate that enhancement of visual or musical abilities is more common in subtypes of fronto-temporal dementia (FTD) that accounts for ~25% of the presenile dementias. In Alzheimer's disease visuoconstructive abilities dissipate in conjunction with the progressive loss of function in posterior parietal and posterior temporal regions, the brain areas responsible for visuoconstructive skills. Contrariwise, in copying skills are often normal and posterior pathology is minimal in FTD. Even though copying skills are preserved, diminished creativity is more common with this illness.

In a recent discussion of the unexpected occurrence of behavioral improvement following brain injury, the term "paradoxical functional facilitation" was used [120]. Whereas "in normal subjects, inhibitory and excitatory mechanisms interact in a complex harmony; the role of inhibitory processes may be critical in mediating specific restorative paradoxical functional facilitation effects". It is well accepted that talent in one area, such as art, may be accompanied by dysfunction in other spheres, such as social skills. The loss of social skills and inhibitions may have facilitated the art of the described patient. The willingness of patient mentioned above to scorn social norms led him to take up painting and quit his work.

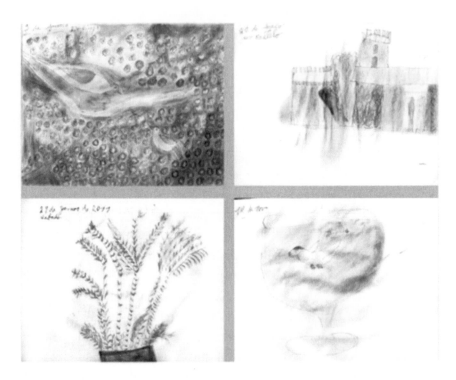

Figure 32. Drawings with higher and lower CAT scores. Left panel: drawings with the highest globalscores (8.5 for the upper drawing, range 4-10; 7.4 for the lower drawing, range 3-10). Right panel: drawings with the lowest global scores (5.8 for the upper drawing, range 4-10; 6.0 for the lower drawing, range2-10) [120].

It may be hypothesized that selective degeneration of the anterior temporal and orbital frontal cortex decreased inhibition of the more posteriorly located visual systems involved with perception, thereby enhancing this patients' artistic interests and abilities. There is an association between bipolar disease and the visual arts, although none of the clinically neurologically reported patients had a history suggestive of mania. A break with social conventions is common among artists and can lead to a freer more creative output. Van Gogh' s and Goya's work blossomed in midlife, when there outsider art spurned conventional rules of society. Artists create distinctive paintings despite receiving little formal training. Some manifest severe mental illness and are hospitalized in mental institutions. Like other psychiatric patients, they are directed internally with little interest in the teachings of others. Some have a history suggesting schizophrenia, but others develop both their talent and a behavioral disorder later in life. Disinhibition, hallucinations, and aphasia are reported in outsider artists. Some may have even suffered from the temporal lobe variant of fronto-temporal dementia [121].

REFERENCES

[1]   T. A. Bahill and L. W. Stark, "Trajectories of saccadic eye movements," *Sci. Am.*, vol. 240, pp. 84–93, 1979.

[2]   M. A. Garcia-Perez and E. Peli, "Intrasaccadic perception," *J. Neurosci.*, vol. 21, no. 18, pp. 7313–7322, 2001.

[3]   T. N. Wiesel and D. H. Hubel, "Receptive fields of cells in striate cortex of very young, visually inexperienced kittens," *J. Neurophysiol.*, vol. 26, pp. 994–1002, 1963.

[4]   T. N. Wiesel and D. H. Hubel, "Receptive fields and functional architecture of monkey striate cortex," *J. Physiol.*, vol. 195, pp. 215–243.

[5]   J. Barners, *The presocratic philosophers*. London and New York: Routledge, 1982.

[6]   G. M. Stratton, "Symmetry, linear illusions and the movements of the eyes," *Psychol. Rev.*, vol. 13, pp. 82–96, 1906.

[7]   H. F. Brandt, "Ocular patterns and their psychological implications.," *Am. J. Psychol.*, vol. 53, pp. 260–268, 1940.

[8]   G. T. Buswell, *How people look at pictures*, 1st ed. Chicago: University of Chicago Press, 1935.

[9]   E. Llewellyn-Thomas, "Movements of the eye," *Sci. Am.*, vol. 219, pp. 88–95, 1968.

[10]   M. Jeannerod, P. Gerin, and J. Pernier, "Deplacements et fixation du regard dans l'exploration libre d'une scene visuelle," *Vision Res.*, vol. 8, pp. 81–97, 1968.

[11] A. Yarbus, *Eye Movements*. Plenum NewYork, 1967.

[12] D. Noton and L. W. Stark, "Scanpaths in eye movements during pattern perception," *Science,*, vol. 171, pp. 308–311, 1971.

[13] D. Noton and L. W. Stark, "Scanpaths in saccadic eye movements while viewing and recognizing patterns," *Vis. Res.*, vol. 11, pp. 929–942, 1971.

[14] T. Ogawa and H. Komatsu, "Target selection in area V4 during a multidimensional visual search task," *J. Neurosci.*, vol. 24, pp. 6371–6382, 2004.

[15] S. Yantis and J. Jonides, "Uniqueness of abrupt visual onset in capturing attention," *Percept. Psychophys.*, vol. 43, pp. 346–354, 1988.

[16] A. V. Belopolsky, L. Zwaan, J. Theeuwes, and A. Kramer, "The size of an attentional window modulates attentional capture by color singletons," *Psychon. Bull. Rev.*, vol. 14, no. 5, pp. 934–938, 2007.

[17] J. Theeuwes, "Top-down search strategies cannot override attentional capture," *Psychon. Bull. Rev.*, vol. 11, no. 65–70, 2004.

[18] I. Biederman, R. J. Mezzanotte, and J. C. Rabinowitz, "Scene perception: detecting and judging objects undergoing relational violations," *Cogn. Psychol.*, vol. 14, pp. 143–177, 1982.

[19] S. Palmer, "Visual perception and world knowledge: notes on a model of sensory-cognitive interaction," in *Explorations in Cognition*, D. A. Norman and D. E. Rumelhart, Eds. Freeman, San Francisco, 1975, pp. 279–307.

[20] M. C. Potter, "Meaning in visual search," *Science,*, vol. 14, no. 187, pp. 965–966, 1975.

[21] L. W. Stark and G. C. Theodoridis, "On the biospheric relevance of information," *Math. Biosci.*, vol. 11, pp. 31–45, 1971.

[22] R. A. Andersen and R. M. Siegel, "Motion processing in primate cortex," in *Signal and sense: local and global order in perceptual maps*, G. Edelman, W. Gall, and W. M. Cowan, Eds. New York: Wiley, 1988, pp. 163–184.

[23] R. Andersen, "Coordinate transformations and motor planning in PPC," in *The Cogmitive Neuroscience*, M. S. Gazzaniga, Ed. MIT Press, Cambridge, 1995, pp. 519–532.

[24] A. M. Silito, H. E. Jones, L. G. Gerstein, and D. C. West, "Feature - linked synchronisation of thalamic relay cell firing induced by feedback from the visual cortex," *Nature*, vol. 369, pp. 479–482, 1994.

[25] K. H. Pribram, *Languages of the brain*. Prentice-Hall, Englewood Cliffs, NJ, 1971.

[26] J. A. Assad and J. H. Maunsell, "Neuronal correlates of inferred motion in primate posterior parietal cortex," *Nature*, vol. 373, pp. 518–520, 1995.

[27] D. N. Rushton, J. C. Rothwell, and M. D. Craggs, "Gating of somatosensory evoked potentials during different kinds of movement in man," *Brain*, vol. 104, no. 3, pp. 465–491, 1981.

[28] C. E. Chapman, W. Jiang, and Y. Lamarre, "Modulation of lemniscal input during conditioned arm movements in the monkey," *Exp. Brain Res.*, vol. 72, pp. 316–334, 1988.

[29] B. Libet, "Conscious vs neural time," *Nature*, vol. 352, no. 6330, pp. 27–28, 1991.

[30] P. E. Roland, "Cortical regulation of selective attention in man," *J. Neurophysiol.*, vol. 48, pp. 1059–1078, 1982.

[31] E. Protter, *Painters on painting*. Courier Corporation, 1971.

[32] G. Brett, *Force fields: phases of the kinetic*. Barcelona: Hayward Gallery, Museu d'Art Contemporani, 2000.

[33] D. Noton and L. W. Stark, "Eye movements and visual perception," *Sci. Am.*, vol. 244, pp. 34–53, 1972.

[34] L. W. Stark, C. M. Privitera, H. Yang, M. Azzariti, Y. F. Ho, T. Blackmon, and D. Chernyak, "Representation of human vision in the brain: How does human perception recognize images?," *J. Electron. Imaging*, vol. 10, no. 1, p. 123, 2001.

[35] J. Y. Lettvin, H. R. Maturana, W. S. McCulloch, and W. H. Pitts, "What the frog's eye tells the frog's brain," *Proc. Inst. Radio Engr.*, vol. 47, pp. 1940–1951, 1959.

[36] D. Gagnon, G. A. O'Driscoll, M. Petrides, and G. B. Pike, "The effect of spatial and temporal information on saccades and neural activity in oculomotor structures," *Brain*, vol. 125, pp. 123–139, 2002.

[37] L. W. Stark, G. Vossius, and L. R. Young, "Predictive control of eye tracking movements," *IEEE Trans. Hum. Fac. Electron. HFE*, vol. 3, pp. 52–67, 1962.

[38] L. W. Stark, W. H. Zangemeister, J. Edwards, J. Grinberg, A. Jones, S. Lehman, P. Lubock, V. Narayan, and M. Nystrom, "Head rotation trajectories compared with eye saccades by main sequence relationships," *Invest. Ophthalmol. Vis. Sci.*, vol. 19, no. 8, pp. 986–988, 1980.

[39] I. Pollack, "Computer simulation of threshold observations by method of limits," *Percept Mot Ski.*, vol. 26, no. 2, pp. 583–586, 1968.

[40] J. Gbadamosi and W. H. Zangemeister, "Visual imagery in hemianopic patients," *J. Cogn. Neurosci.*, vol. 13, no. 7, pp. 855–66, 2001.

[41] S. A. Brandt and L. W. Stark, "Spontaneous eye movements during visual imagery," *J. Cogn Neurosci*, vol. 9, pp. 27–38, 1997.

[42] L. W. Stark, I. Yamashita, G. Tharp, and H. Ngo, "Searchpatterns and searchpaths," in *Visual Search II*, D. Brogan and K. Carr, Eds. Taylor& Francis, 1992, pp. 37–58.

[43] G. Zhou, K. Ezumi, and L. W. Stark, "Efficiency of search patterns," *Comput. Biol. Med.*, vol. 23, pp. 511–524, 1993.

[44] G. Gauthier, P. Mandelbrojt, J. Vercher, E. Marchetti, and G. Obrecht, "Adaptation of the visuo-manual system to optical correction," in *Presbyopia - recent research*, L. W. Stark and G. Obrecht, Eds. Fairchild PUN., N.Y., 1985, pp. 165–171.

[45] L. E. Javal, "Essai sur la physiologie de la lecture," *Ann. Ocul. (Paris).*, vol. 79,79,80, pp. 97–117, 135–147, 240–274, 1878.

[46] N. J. Wade and B. W. Tatler, "Did Javal measure eye movements during reading?," *J. Eye Mov. Res.*, vol. 2, no. 5, pp. 1–7, 2009.

[47] C. M. Privitera, T. Carney, S. Klein, and M. Aguilar, "Analysis of microsaccades and pupil dilation reveals a common decisional origin during visual search," *Vision Res.*, vol. 95, pp. 43–50, 2014.

[48] D. Ballard, M. Hayhoe, and J. Pelz, "Memory representations in natural tasks," *J. Cogn. Neurosci.*, vol. 7, pp. 66–68, 1995.

[49] M. M. Hayhoe, D. H. Ballard, and S. D. Whitehead, "Memory use during hand-eye coordination," *Proc. Cogn. Sci. Soc.*, vol. 15, pp. 534–536, 1993.

[50] C. M. Privitera, T. Fujita, D. Chernyak, and L. W. Stark, "On the discriminability of hROIs, human visually selected regions-of-interest," *Biol. Cybern.*, vol. 93, no. 2, pp. 141–152, 2005.

[51] S. M. Kosslyn, *Image and brain: The resolution of the imagery debate*. Cambridge, MA: MIT Press, 1994.

[52] J. Kamiya, "Behavioral, subjective, and physiological aspects of sleep," in *Functions of varied experience*, D. W. Fidke and S. R. Maddi, Eds. Homewood, Illinois: Dorsey Press, 1961, pp. 145–174.

[53] S. M. Kosslyn, "Scanning visual images: Some structural implications," *Percept. Psychophys.*, vol. 14, pp. 90–94, 1973.

[54] R. A. Finke and S. Pinker, "Spontaneous imagery scanning in mental extrapolation," *J. Exp. Psychol. Learn. Mem. Cogn.*, vol. 8, pp. 142–147, 1982.

[55] S. M. Kosslyn, "Measuring the visual angle of the mind's eye," *Cogn. Psychol.*, vol. 10, no. 3, pp. 356–389, 1978.

[56] S. R. Ellis and L. W. Stark, "Eye movements during the viewing of Necker cubes," *Perception*, vol. 7, no. 5, pp. 575–581, 1978.

[57] R. N. Shepard and J. Metzler, "Mental rotation of three-dimensional objects," *Science,*, vol. 171, no. 972, pp. 701–703, 1971.

[58] L. A. Cooper, "Mental rotation of random two-dimensional shapes," *Cogn. Psychol.*, vol. 7, pp. 20–43, 1975.

[59] R. A. Finke and M. Schmidt, "Orientation specific color aftereffects following imagination," *J. Exp. Psychol. Hum. Percept. Perform.*, vol. 3, pp. 599–606, 1977.

[60] W. H. Zangemeister and U. Oechsner, "Evidence for scanpaths in hemianopic patients shown through string editing methods.," in *Attention and Cognition*, WH Zangemeister SS Stiehl C Freksa, Ed. Oxford Amsterdam: Elsevier, 1996, pp. 196–226.

[61] W. Zangemeister, "Evidence for a global scanpath strategy in viewing abstract compared with realistic images," *Neuropsychologia*, vol. 33, no. 8, pp. 1009–1025, 1995.

[62] L. W. Stark and S. Ellis, "Scanpath revisited: Cognitive models in active looking," in *Eye Movements.*, M. R. Fisher, DF and S. JW:, Eds. Hillsdale, N.J: Erlbaum Ass., 1981, pp. 193–226.

[63] R. Groner, F. Walder, and M. Groen, "Looking at faces: Local and global aspects of scanpaths," *Adv. Psychol.*, vol. 22, pp. 523–533, 1982.

[64] R. A. Finke, *Principles of mental imagery.* Cambridge, MA: MIT Press, 1989.

[65] G. A. Carpenter, S. Grossberg, and G. W. Lesher, "The what-and-where filter. A spatial mapping neural network for object recognition and image understanding," *Comput. Vis. Image Underst.*, vol. 69, no. 1, pp. 1–22, 1998.

[66] W. H. Zangemeister, K. Sherman, and L. W. Stark, "Evidence for a global scanpath strategy in viewing abstract compared with realistic images," *Neuropsychologia*, vol. 33, no. 8, pp. 1009–1025, 1995.

[67] N. Koide, T. Kubo, S. Nishida, T. Shibata, and K. Ikeda, "Art Expertise Reduces Influence of Visual Salience on Fixation in Viewing Abstract-Paintings," *PLoS One*, vol. 10, no. 2, p. e0117696, 2015.

[68] M. Jeannerod, "Mechanisms of visuomotor coordination: a study in normal and brain-damaged subjects," *Neuropsychologia*, vol. 24, pp. 41–78, 1986.

[69] W. H. Zangemeister and U. Oechsner, "Adaptation to visual field defects with virtual reality," in *Current Oculomotor Research*, W. Becker, H. Deubel, and T. Mergner, Eds. Kluwer, NY, 1999, pp. 89–95.

[70] W. H. Zangemeister and P. Utz, "An increase in a virtual hemianopic field defect enhances the efficiency of secondary adaptive gaze strategies," *Cah. Psychol. Cogn. Psychol. Cogn.*, vol. 21, no. 2–3, pp. 281–303, 2002.

[71] C. F. Nodine, P. J. Locher, and E. A. Krupinski, "The role of formal art training perception and aesthetic judgment of art compositions," *Leonardo*, vol. 26, no. 3, pp. 219–227, 1993.

[72] N. H. Mackworth and A. J. Morandi, "The gaze selects informative details within picture," *Percept. Psychophys.*, vol. 2, no. 11, pp. 547–552, 1967.

[73] J. Zihl, "Visual scanning behavior in patients with homonymous hemianopia," *Neuropsychologia*, vol. 33, pp. 287–303, 1995.

[74] C. D. Gilbert, "Circuitry, architecture and functional dynamics of visual cortex," *Cereb. Cortex*, vol. 3, pp. 373–386, 1993.

[75] V. S. Ramachandran, "Behavioral and magnetoencephalographic correlates of plasticity in the adult human brain," *Proc. Natl. \ Acad. Sci. USA*, vol. 90, no. 22, pp. 10413–10420, 1993.

[76] D. E. Berlyne, *Aesthetics and psychobiology*. New York: Appleton-Century- Crofts, 1971.

[77] V. S. Ramachandran and R. L. Gregory, "Perceptual filling in of artificially induced scotomas in human vision," *Nature*, vol. 350, no. 6320, pp. 699–702, 1991.

[78] R. W. Ditchburn, *Eye movements and visual perception*. Clarendon Press, Oxford, 1973.

[79] A. M. Treisman and G. Gelade, "A feature-integration theory of attention," *Cogn. Psychol.*, vol. 12, no. 1, pp. 97–136, 1980.

[80] W. Reichardt, "On optical resolving ability of the facet eye of Limulus," *Kybernetik.*, vol. 1, pp. 57–69, 1961.

[81] U. Neisser, *Cognition and reality: Principles and implications of cognitive psychology*. WH Freeman, San Francisco, 1976.

[82] M. Farah, "Psychophysical evidence for a shared representational medium for mental images and percepts," *J. Exp. Psychol. Gen.*, vol. 114, pp. 91–103, 1985.

[83] D. Marschalek and F. Neperud, "The National Gallery of Art Laserdisk and accompanying database: A means to enhance art instruction.," *Art Educ.*, vol. 44, no. 3, pp. 48–53, 1983.

[84] F. Molnar, "About the role of visual exploration," in *Intrinsic motivation and aesthetics.*, Hy Day, Ed. New York: Plenum, 1981, pp. 385–414.

[85] F. Molnar, "Perception visuelle de l'unite," 1974.

[86] R. L. J. Solso, "The cognitive neuroscience of art," *J. Conscious. Stud.*, vol. 7, no. 8–9, pp. 75–85, 2000.

[87] M. Corbetta, F. M. Miezin, S. Dobmeyer, G. L. Shulman, and S. E. Petersen, "Selective and divided attention during visual discriminations of shape, color, and speed: Functional anatomy by positron emission tomography," *J. Neurosci.*, vol. 11, pp. 2382–2402, 1991.

[88] J. Moran and R. Desimone, "Selective attention gates visual processing in the extrastriate cortex," *Science,*, vol. 229, pp. 782–784, 1985.

[89] J. A. Brefczynski and E. A. DeYoe, "A physiological correlate of the 'spotlight' of visual attention," *Nat. Neurosci.*, vol. 2, no. 4, pp. 370–374, 1999.

[90] M. S. Aldrich, A. G. Beck, and S. Gilman, "Cortical blindness: etiology, diagnostic, and prognosis," *Ann. Neurol.*, vol. 21, pp. 149–158, 1987.

[91] J. J. S. Barton and J. Sharpe, "Smooth pursuit and saccades to moving targets in blind hemifields A comparison of medial occipital, lateral occipital and optic radiation lesions," pp. 681–699, 1997.

[92] W. H. Merigan and J. H. R. Maunsell, "How parallel are the primate visual pathways?," *Annu. Rev. Neurosci.*, vol. 16, no. 369–402, 1993.

[93] P. De Weerd, R. Gattass, R. Desimone, and L. G. Ungerleider, "Responses of cells in monkey visual cortex during perceptual fillingin of an artificial scotoma," *Nature*, vol. 377, pp. 731–734, 1995.

[94] G. Beckers and V. Hoemberg, "Impairment of visual perception and visual short term memory scanning by transcranial magnetic stimulation of occipital cortex," *Exp. Brain Res.*, vol. 87, no. 2, pp. 421–432, 1991.

[95] G. Wunderlich, B. Suchan, J. Volkmann, H. Herzog, V. Homberg, R. Seitz, and J, "Visual hallucinations in recovery from cortical blindness: Imaging correlates," *Arch. Neurol.*, vol. 57, pp. 561–565, 2000.

[96] J. Elderfield, "Seeing bonnard," in *S. Bonnard Retrospective*, Whitfield D. & J. Elderfield, Ed. New York: The museum of Modern Art, 1998, pp. 33–52.

[97] C. Privitera, W. H. Zangemeister, and L. W. Stark, "Bonnard's representation of the perception of substance," *J. Eye Mov. Reseach*, vol. 1, no. 1, pp. 1–6, 2007.

[98] I. Sandler and O. Greenberg, "Art from the late 1960s to the early 1990s," in *Art of the Postmodern Era*, I. Sandler, Ed. New York: Icon Editions, Harper & Collins N.Y., 1996, p. 332-375.

[99] O. G. Selfridge, *The mechanization of thought processes*. London: HM Stationery Office, 1959.

[100] D. Navon, "Forest before trees: The precedence of global features in visual perception," *Cogn. Psychol.*, vol. 9, pp. 353–383, 1977.

[101] J. B. Hellige, "Behavioral and brain asymmetries in nonhuman species," in *Hemispheric asymmetry: what's right and what's left*, J. B. Hellige, Ed. Cambridge (MA): Harvard University Press, 1993, pp. 136–167.

[102] C. Krischer and W. H. Zangemeister, "Scanpaths in reading and picture viewing: Computer-assisted optimization of display conditions," *Comput. Biol. Med.*, vol. 37, pp. 947 – 956, 2007.

[103] L. R. Young and L. W. Stark, "Variable feedback experiments testing a sampled data model for eye tracking movements," *IEEE Trans. Hum. Factors Electron.*, vol. 4, pp. 38–51, 1963.

[104] G. W. Humphreys, M. J. Riddoch, P. T. Quinlan, C. J. Price, and N. Donnelly, "Parallel pattern processing in visual agnosia," *Can. J. Psychol.*, vol. 46, pp. 377–416, 1992.

[105] M. I. Posner and S. E. Petersen, "The attention system of the human brain," *Annu. Rev. Neurosci.*, vol. 13, pp. 25–42, 1990.

[106] B. Dubois and B. Pillon, "Cognitive deficits in Par- kinson's disease," *J. Neurol.*, vol. 244, pp. 2–8, 1997.

[107] U. Sabatini, K. Boulanouar, N. Fabre, F. Martin, C. Carel, C. Colonnese, L. Bozzao, I. Berry, J. L. Montastruc, F. Chollet, and O. Rascol, "Cortical motor reorganization in akinetic patients with Parkinson's disease: a functional MRI study," *Brain*, vol. 123, pp. 394–403, 2000.

[108] C. Buhmann, F. Binkofski, C. Klein, C. Büchel, C. van Eimeren, T., Erdmann, K. Hedrich, M. Kasten, J. Hagenah, G. Deuschl, P. P. Pramstaller, and H. R. Siebner, "Motor reorganization in asymptomatic carriers of a single mutant Parkin allele: a human model for presymptomatic parkinsonism," *Brain*, vol. 128, pp. 2281–2290, 2005.

[109] J. Mink, "The basal ganglia: focused selection and inhibition of competing motor programs," *Prog. Neurobiol.*, vol. 50, pp. 381–425, 1996.

[110] F. Chan, I. T. Armstrong, G. Pari, R. J. Riopelle, and D. P. Munoz, "Deficits in saccadic eye-movement control in Parkin- son's disease," *Neuropsychologia*, vol. 43, pp. 784–796, 2005.

[111] S. Colnaghi, G. Beltrami, A. Cortese, W. H. Zangemeister, V. Cosi, and M. Versino, "Multiple memory-guided saccades: movement memory improves the accuracy of memory-guided saccades," *Prog. Brain Res. Brain Res*, vol. 171, pp. 425–427, 2008.

[112] C. Maioli, I. Benaglio, S. Siri, K. Sosta, and S. Cappa, "The integration of parallel and serial processing mechanisms in visual search: evidence from eye movement recording," *Eur. Neurosci.*, vol. 13, pp. 364–372, 2001.

[113] M. J. Farah, M. J. Soso, and R. M. Dasheiff, "Visual angle of the mind's eye before and after unilateral occipital lobectomy," *J. Exp. Psychol. Hum. Perception&Performance*, vol. 18, no. 1, pp. 241–246, 1992.

[114] S. M. Kosslyn, A. Pascual-Leone, O. Felician, S. Camposano, J. P. Keenan, W. L. Thompson, G. Ganis, K. E. Sukel, and N. M. Alpert, "The role of area 17 in visual imagery: convergent evidence from PET and rTMS," *Science,*, vol. 284, no. 5411, pp. 167–170, 1999.

[115] G. Deutsch, W. T. Bourbon, and A. C. Papanicolaou, "Visuospatial tasks compared via activation of regional cerebral blood flow," *Neuropsychologia*, vol. 26, no. 3, pp. 445–452, 1988.

[116] W. Schneider, D. C. Noll, and J. D. Cohen, "Functional topographic mapping of the cortical ribbon in human vision with conventional MRI scanners," *Nature*, vol. 365, no. 6442, pp. 150–53, 1993.

[117] L. C. de Souza, H. C. Guimarães, A. L. Teixeira, P. Caramelli, R. Levy, B. Dubois, and E. Volle, "Frontal lobe neurology and the creative mind," *Front. Psychol.*, vol. 23, no. 5, p. 761, 2014.

[118] V. B. Buren, B. Bromberger, D. Potts, B. Miller, and A. Chatterjee, "Changes in painting styles of two artists with Alzheimer's disease," *Psychol. Aesthetics, Creat., Arts*, vol. 7, p. 89–94, 2013.

[119] K. P. Rankin, A. A. Liu, S. Howard, H. Slama, C. E. Hou, K. Shuster, and B. L. Miller, "A case-controlled study of altered visual art production in Alzheimer's and FTLD," *Cogn. Behav. Neurol.*, vol. 20, no. 1, pp. 48–61, 2007.

[120] L. C. de Souza, H. C. Guimarães, A. L. Teixeira, P. Caramelli, R. Levy, B. Dubois, and E. Volle, "Frontal lobe neurology and the creative mind," *Front. Psychol.*, vol. 5, p. 761, 2014.

[121] B. Brand-Clausen and T. Roeske, Eds., "Prinzhorn Collection," in *Artists off the rails*, Wunderhorn Publ. Heidelberg, 2008.

Chapter 3

ART AS A FORM OF COMMUNICATION

Anticipation/prediction in gaze-eye and head movements and the concatenation of sequences of fixations when executing scanpaths to input pictures and dynamic scenes governs our perception and understanding of visual art. Claude Shannon's information theory explains the exchange of information between the artist and viewer, that is embedded in a more subjective, local, regional, and nowadays global context concerning perception and expectation of art. Information theory is therefore the matrix into which to embed the top down active vision scanpath theory. Knowing and using the top down approach will bestow a more refined way to view, recognize and finally perceive different works of art as messages of artistic models. It enables the viewer to be more aware and apply consciously his personal, subjective models of works of art. Message-channel-corruption happens in painting as coding and embedding. The just noticeable differences in the shade of a pixel and the resolution available in the receiver's strongly limits the amount of information about an image that can be sensed. Therefore, the information received by the retinal and cortical mechanisms is usually much less than the original image. In his introduction to information-theory and aesthetics Max Bense notes that semiotically speaking, every measure implies a reference to an object;

every value implies a reference to an interpretant. Therefore in principle, creative communication and evaluative communication are separate phases of a process that produces art. In reality they are superimposed on each other all the time, since every creative act in the sense of producing innovations is made up of partial creations, interspersed with judgments, acts of acceptance or dismissal.

1. THE ARTIST AS SENDER OF A COMMUNICATION

a. Gaze Anticipation While Executing Scanpaths

The visual system, particularly gaze movements guide our behaviour in natural environments. Many animals including humans have evolved a non-homogeneous retina to optimize information transmission and serially sample visual scenes by saccadic eye movements. Such gaze movements introduce high-speed retinal motion and decouple external and internal reference frames. It has been demonstrated that perceptual decisions can be made in world that is gaze-, rather than retinal- coordinates. Gaze saccades, very fast movements, are more often than not synkinetic coordinated fast eye and – frequently slow – head movements. This means their internal latencies within the central nervous system must be flexible, due to:

i.   *anticipation*-prediction of the subject;
ii. *randomness* of internal and environmental stimuli;
iii. *dynamic differences* and limitations of the fast eye compared to the slower head movements.

Anticipation-prediction plays a major role for saccadic gaze movements. It permits us to find one or more targets of interest; we can connect multiple targets within a region of interest, a ROI, through concatenation of sequences of fixations to "view" and understand a picture. These sequences are called scanpaths [1, 2]. Their characteristics in space and time are defined by the subject's top down predictive knowledge of the environment, or a particular scene/picture. Bottom-up mechanisms are interwoven in this process such that a picture may – to some extent – influence the sequence of fixations. In normal life, pictures are most often dynamic scenes rather than static two- or three-dimensional pictures. Gaze fixations occurring during dynamic visual input are therefore performed through smooth pursuit gaze movements and gaze saccades. Under natural conditions, visual sensitivity during gaze saccades is reduced. This is due to high retinal speed during a saccade – also true for microsaccades: With or without recourse to an extra-retinal mechanism of active suppression is still debated. Gaze coordination of eye and head, extending between total prediction and pure randomness is the most important factor when executing scanpaths to input pictures and dynamic scenes. Fixational micro-eye-movements, in particular microsaccades, contribute to perception and intimate understanding of fixation of static pictures [3, 4].

b. Claude Shannon's Information Theory – The Matrix: Relationship between Art, Neuroscience, and Information Theory

Links between art and science exist and have existed for a long time. An early example was Leonardo's research on optics, the perspective and colour vision. David Hockney has remarked [5] that in the 16th and 17th century many artists tried to "copy nature" through the use of optical instruments like magnifying lenses and other recently developed optical devices. The veracity of such a claim is open to question – but cooperation between the world of psychophysics and art has been historically demonstrated, being embodied by the embracement of contemporary research into physiological optics by the impressionist painters. More recently, artists have used techniques developed in applied science, such as CT-scan radiographs or MRI scans of the brain, for artistic pictorial purposes, whilst others have exploited the digital world of moving pictures and animation. The pitfalls of pure bottom-up explanations of how we look at art are obvious. Without possessing a model or preconception concerning the implications of a painting – be them religious, semantic, historical, sociological, political or technical – the viewer will never be able to detect, appreciate or perceive the "true message" of the painting with any clarity. However, despite an absence of specific prior knowledge, that he often may not be aware of, in many instances this viewer would still be able to match the pictorial content with his common knowledge of the world. Again, this would still not symbolize a true viewing from bottom-up. Rather, it would embody a more simplistic, less sophisticated application of top down viewing of that painting. A complete bottom-up viewing of figurative artistic pictures is hardly conceivable: The non–sophisticated, naive observer of art would still implement rudimentary models of how pictures should and in fact could look like, using preconceived knowledge stemming from "realistic and naturalistic" views of the environment.

The viewer would be lost – as in fact many are – with abstract conceived paintings by Malevich, Rothko or Pollock – even though he might appreciate shapes and colors of these paintings. This is increasingly valid for recent conceptual artworks. In the case of a more primarily "abstract" painting, e.g., a Rothko painting, there could be a more fundamental, bottom-up like processing of the picture: although it is likely that the naive viewer would persistently endeavor to apply known shapes or patterns in a top down fashion. Some believe there may be a universal "sense of beauty". This may be true with respect to universal "primitives" such as symmetry, geometrical shapes, or general face perception – as we now know from neuroimaging studies. However, this kind of "sense of beauty" is heavily influenced by our preconceptions, expectations, and therefore also by cultural and historical differences of artist and viewer. (For an extended comment on this problem see Zeki [6].) Our view concerning the exchange of information between the artist and viewer, is embedded in a more subjective, local, regional, and nowadays global context concerning perception and expectation of art. Information theory is clearly the matrix into which we would like to embed our top down active vision scanpath theory, but how can we achieve this?

The question arises: What is so specific about the top down versus bottom-up information-seeking process when viewing art? What distinguishes it from everyday visual perception? Framing the processes of vision, cognition and perception within "new neurology" and information theory – which brings together and systemizes many facts known from neurology and psychology – may aid viewers be them specialists or naive. It enables them to *be more aware and apply consciously their personal, subjective models of works of art.* Knowing and using the top down approach in this case will bestow a more refined way to view, recognize and finally perceive different works of art as messages of artistic models. The viewer will be more conscious of his own limited way of viewing artworks. Making allowances for some fuzziness in the "signal to noise level", this approach may unveil exactly "what" the artist really means to convey in pictorial form. With his more conscious explication of the workings of top down and bottom-up mechanisms in this recognition process, he will be able to better follow the intentions of a given painting.

c. The Artistic Process of Communication

What is a Picture? A *picture*, is some localized sub-region of a broad scene, with a frame of peripheral content, and perhaps with related objects, that can be modelled in a top down fashion and checked with the high-resolution fovea. A more focused and framed picture could be an *art picture*. It is a constructed use of factual material, wherein the construction is a work of art. This is relevant to the artist attempting to communicate through a painting or, sculpture, installation etc. The artist's painting begins with his model of related objects within a frame, that carry a story either classically in representative art, or a story in terms of artistic technology, or in terms of certain phases of abstract art. Other phases, of course, combine these.

Does the artist lead the viewer's eye?

When the artist paints in order to see: Does the artist lead the eye of the viewer? E. Gombrich [7] opposes the critics, who like to tell us how the artist "leads the eye".

"We believe that we take in the picture more or less at one glance and recognize the motif. Critics like to tell us how the artist "leads the eye" along the main lines of his composition. But our roving eyes will not be thus "led". The critic's phrase should have become obsolete, as it is misleading, since eye movements have been recorded and filmed and the sequential fixation points plotted on top of pictures. These records confirm what Escher made us suspect: reading a picture is a piecemeal affair that starts with random shots and these are followed by the search for a coherent whole. The picture becomes a picture only if the marks on the paper are sorted out by the mind into a consistent and coherent message." Many people use their unimpaired sense of sight to no better advantage during much of the day. But vision is active exploration, obviously seeing can mean more than that. The physicists' definition of the optical process prescribes that light is emitted or reflected by objects in the environment and the lenses of the eye project images of these objects onto the retinas, which transmit the message to the brain. "The reading of pictures must follow a similar pattern as in reading a familiar language. But once we set out to discover how we read the "score", in particular how we have to revise our expectations, we become aware of the part which assumptions play in the reading of images" [8]. Except for the initial glance at a picture of perhaps one second, viewing is an active exploration.

R. Arnheim [9] started an important argument in favour of vision as active exploration. From a negative position he was saying, that from the description of the physiological mechanisms one may be tempted to infer that the correlated processes of shape perception are almost wholly passive and proceed in linear fashion from the registering of the smallest elements to the compounding of larger units. However he explains that both these assumptions are misleading: The world of images does not simply imprint itself upon a faithfully sensitive organ, since in looking at an object, we actively reach out for it.

"With an invisible finger, we move through the space around us, go out to the distant places where things are found, touch them, catch them, scan their surfaces, trace their borders, explore their texture. Therefore, perceiving shapes is an highly active occupation. Primitive optics and the experience from which it sprang became explicit in poetical description."

Like T. S. Eliot wrote: "And the unseen eyebeam crossed, for the roses had the look of flowers that are looked at" (cit. after Arnheim). If an observer intently examines an object, he finds his eyes well equipped to see minute detail. However, visual perception does not operate with the mechanical faithfulness of a camera, which records everything impartially. But what do we see when we see? Certainly not all the innumerable elements of information, rather some of them:

"Seeing means grasping some outstanding features of objects – the blueness of the sky, the curve of the swan's neck, the rectangularity of the book, the sheen of a piece of metal, the straightness of the cigarette. A few simple lines and dots are readily accepted as a "face", not only by civilized Westerners, who may be suspected of having agreed among one another on such "sign language", but also by babies, savages, and animals".

Therefore the conclusion is: Vision is an active grasp of the essentials, it tries to take hold of the basic visual features and their relationships.

The artistic process in light of Shannon's Theory of Communication [10] is depicted in the following Figure 33 (modified from [11]). The picture created by the artist is the information source or message that is coded by style, history, subjective perception, social relations etc. and transmitted through the information channel (vision, but also written explanations etc.). In this process limited channel capacity and bit rate, plus external noise may change, even disrupt the original message. Decoding the received signal may be insufficient, in spite of error correction and bit checking, such that the receiver/spectator might understand the artist's message or may not – due to the above limitations.

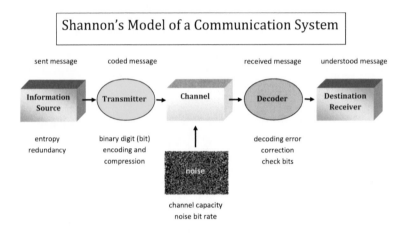

Figure 33. The artistic process and Shannon's Theory of Communication.

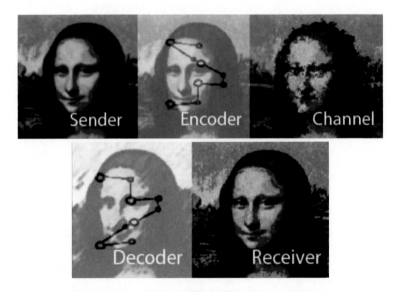

Figure 34. Illustration showing partial image and scanpath corruption due to limited bit rate, channel capacity and noise [12].

When we view a painting, our eye focuses on curves, angles, line crossings, shadows, colours. In the bottom-up scheme, the viewer follows the given basic stimuli and cues like the drop of a line or the red of a peaked angle. In the top down scheme, the viewer uses a set of pre-existent models, which one could optimally match the picture one is looking at. While the matching process is going on between the viewer's internal model and the picture, there is a continuous exchange between top down and bottom-up. In both cases we are looking at the painting or any object over some period of time. Thus, we can fixate on objects or regions of interest only in sequence, such that duration of these fixations becomes an important parameter, since during longer lasting fixations of small areas most of the picture's detailed information is taken in. In Figure 34, this process is depicted in terms of Shannon's theory.

A picture of art may be the complex message – perhaps confounded by unfocussed ideas and unclear representations of the artist – that the artist-sender has imagined using sets of imagery scanpaths, and encoded with his technique and skill.

Shannon worked in many areas, most notably in information theory, a development which was published in 1948 as "A Mathematical Theory of Communication" [10]. In this paper, it was shown that all information sources – telegraph keys, people speaking, television cameras and so on – have a "source rate" associated with them, which can be measured in bits per second. Communication channels have a "capacity" measured in the same units. The information can be transmitted over the channel if, and only if, the source rate does not exceed the channel capacity. This work on communication is generally considered to be Shannon's most important scientific contribution. In 1981 Professor Irving Reed, speaking at the International Symposium on Information Theory in Brighton, England, said:

"It was thirty-three years ago, in 1948, that Professor Claude E. Shannon first published his uniquely original paper, "A Mathematical Theory of Communication," in the Bell System Technical Journal. Few other works of this century have had greater impact on science and engineering. By this landmark paper and his several subsequent papers on information theory he has altered most profoundly all aspects of communication theory and practice."

To give one a flavor of how we continue to use and think in terms of the cybernetic revolution, let us consider the amount of information in a digital image. It is limited by its resolution or number of pixels, each considered as an informational symbol. Each pixel in turn is specified by a certain number of gray levels (perhaps to 8 bits precision) or of trichromatic color levels (perhaps to 24 bits) that enter into Shannon's formula as a logarithmic term. The product of the log of the number of gray levels times the number of pixels gives the total informational content of a digital image in bits. If the sampling is sufficient any analog image is completely transformed into a digital image – clearly in the noisy universe in which we are immersed, there cannot be an infinite amount of information in any analog value. Of course, the information received by the retinal and cortical mechanisms is usually much less than the original image. The "jnd's" or just noticeable differences in the shade of a pixel and the resolution available in the receivers strongly limits the amount of information about an image that can be sensed. This is now an active area in the study of engineering image compression and indeed of vision.

Painting as coding and embedding of information and channel corruption: The spectator is actively looking

Marcel Duchamp said:

"the spectator is actively looking ... art is a drug: Art has absolutely no existence as veracity, as truth. The onlooker is important as the artist." This is another, perhaps the first and one of the best direct examples of the usage of explicit description of the artist and the viewer communicating through a work of art. "In the creative act, the artist goes from intention to realization through a chain of totally subjective reactions. His struggle toward the realization is a series of efforts, pains, satisfactions, refusals and decisions, which also cannot and must not be fully self-conscious, at least on the aesthetic plane. The result of this struggle is a difference between the intention and its realization, a difference which the artist is not aware of [13].

Consequently, in the chain of reactions accompanying the creative act, a link is missing. This gap which represents the inability of the artist to express fully his intention; this difference between what he intended to realize and did realize, is the personal "art coefficient" contained in the work. In other words, the personal "art coefficient" is like an arithmetical relation between the unexpressed but intended and the unintentionally expressed. To avoid a misunderstanding, we must remember that this "art coefficient" is a personal expression of art that is, still in a raw state, which must be "refined" as pure sugar from molasses, by the spectator; the digit of this coefficient has no bearing whatsoever on his verdict. The creative act takes another aspect when the spectator experiences the phenomenon of transmutation; through the change from inert matter into a work of art, an actual transubstantiation has taken place, and the role of the spectator is to determine the weight of the work on the esthetic scale."

All in all, the creative act is not performed by the artist alone; the spectator brings the work in contact with the external world by deciphering and interpreting its inner qualifications and thus adds his contribution to the creative act. "This becomes even more obvious when posterity gives its final verdict and sometimes rehabilitates forgotten artists." This is another, perhaps the first and one of the best direct examples of the usage of explicit description of the artist and the viewer communicating through a work of art. And the spectator is "actively looking" [13].

Duchamp makes it clear that he is not interested in explicating and analyzing pictures. The imponderable statement of pictures, sculptures and objects – the fabrication of novel references, turn out to be more important than definitive explications of pictures. When looking for a pattern for the interpretive maelstrom into which Duchamp has thrown us, he is master of a technique of interpretation which is capable of refuting any contradiction, any skepticism like the moustache which the Frenchman adds to the Mona Lisa. Everything that Duchamp did was based on an appeal to commentary and calculation. A merely formal, phenomenological reflection of ready-mades and their equation with sculpture was therefore out of the question for him.

Figure 35. Duchamp: left, "Nude descending a Staircase No.2", 1912; right, "Bicycle Wheel", 1913.

d. Message Channel Corruption and Painting as Coding and Embedding

Shannon's noiseless feedback theorem states that even if one were to have noiseless feedback from receiver to sender, this would not incur an increase in channel capacity! What advantage then can noiseless feedback provide? Kailath and Schalwijck [14] have provided a specific situation to exemplify this idea. A satellite orbits Jupiter and transmits pictures of Jupiter's surface back to Earth; it has limited power and antenna size, and thus signal strength is weak. The noisy channel between Jupiter and Earth consists of cosmic rays and solar wind. The Earth antenna is large and power is essentially unlimited; this is the noiseless feedback. Now, although noiseless feedback cannot increase channel capacity, it can reduce the complexity of the code that achieves capacity. In this way, e.g., by sending back the received picture to be checked against the uncorrupted sent picture, the satellite need only send a few bits of information to correct the errors in transmission. Thus more correct pictures can be received per unit time over the same channel. Let us suppose that Adam Sillito's [15] neurophysiological observations of a feedback interaction between levels four and six of the visual cortex provides such a potential mechanism. Incoming bottom-up visual information is very limited and noisy; the out-coming top down information of the brain resembles a large antenna and practically unlimited power: noiseless feedback could take place. In terms of neuro-aesthetics this would mean that the artist/sender tries to behave like a large antenna with almost unlimited power using all sorts of public relation resources including the media to send his artistic message to his potential audience. Since he knows that his essential message might be corrupted by inevitable noise, small channel capacity, and errors of decoding – generated amongst others by art critics – he might try to keep the message very simple. So, his audience might "understand" him easier and eventually buy his art. A characteristic approach in this respect is the technique to use museums as amplifiers of so far lesser known works of art.

e. Max Bense - Information Theory and Aesthetics

In his work to information theory and aesthetics Max Bense [16] states that the semiotic and numerical methods of neuro-aesthetics are primarily analytical and descriptive; they are relevant with respect to the object, since analysis and description concern the neuro-aesthetic state as an artistic object. The generative methods, on the other hand, are clearly relevant with respect to the material; they only manipulate the medium, serve material synthesis and construction. Evaluative aesthetics is relevant with respect to the interpretant; it reflects the aesthetic state and views it as a repertoire of its own possibilities, makes another, second selection, as it were, dismisses or acknowledges the object not as such, but as something to be evaluated, and therefore as a value. Semiotically speaking, every measure implies a reference to an object; every value implies a reference to an interpretant. Therefore in principle, creative communication and evaluative communication are separate phases of a process that produces art; in reality they are superimposed on each other all the time, since every creative act in the sense of producing innovations is made up of partial creations, interspersed with judgments, acts of acceptance or dismissal.

The productive phase is thus always accompanied by a phase of reflective consumption; measures are constantly translated into values, so that a schema of neuro-aesthetic communication would be as follows in Figure 36.

> "It is only in the act of judging that the artistic process reaches its communicative end in the consciousness. Consciousness is to be understood as a behavioral system, whereas judging is behavior that translates decisions into actions".

If we split up the semiosis, that is the semiotic process of neuro-aesthetic communication, into its syntactic, semantic and pragmatic phases, the system of degrees of freedom available for neuro-aesthetic decisions during art production reveals a progressive schema as proposed by Bense depicted in Figure 36.

The parts of the semiotic process of aesthetic communication

expedient (material repertoire)	syntactic innovation	aesthetic order (finite schema)
order	semantic innovation	aesthetic representation (concrete or abstract object)
representation	pragmatic innovation	percipient -> value (judging consciousness)

Figure 36. Informational neuro-aesthetic schema and the parts of the semiotic process of neuro-aesthetic communication (M. Bense 1965).

Material system, ordering system, representative system and value system thus follow one from the other. "According to the generative view of the triadic relation of signs, syntactic innovation is the development of the medium; semantic innovation develops the object reference, and pragmatic innovation develops the interpretant." Value is always part of the interpretant's system of reference. Since meanings in the sphere of the interpretant must be seen as encodings of references [in the object domain], and since these encodings are achieved through the communicative function of the media [which in a general model of communication correspond to the channel of communication] the semiotic conception of value can easily be replaced by a numerical or information-theoretical one.

As Duchamp pointed out, the creative act is not performed by the artist alone since:

> "the spectator brings the work in contact with the external world by deciphering and interpreting its inner qualifications and thus adds his contribution to the creative act. This becomes even more obvious when posterity gives its final verdict and sometimes rehabilitates forgotten artists" [13].

Creative communication (artist-sender) and evaluating communication (viewer-receiver) are separate phases of a process that produces art. Evaluative aesthetics is relevant with respect to the interpreter [16].

2. THE VIEWER AS RECEIVER OF A COMMUNICATION

How do viewers receive the painting's message? Similarly as the artist and his artwork's viewer, in visual science and art each is attempting to communicate mental images through patterns, structures and forms; they also change the object of interest through observation and perception in the qualitative domain of cognition and in the quantitative domain of measurements. Visual science and art can therefore be regarded each as a mode of communication of mental imagery by pattern or structure in some selected medium. Objects-as-seen were distinguished from objects-in-the-world, when men have formulated theories of their relation. This theme runs through the development of the science of geometrical optics. It has been influential in guiding research in the anatomy and physiology of the visual receptors and their projections in the brain, and it remains with us in contemporary formulations of the psychology of perception. Successful art changes our understanding of the conventions by altering our perceptions. Perception of ideas leads to new ideas. The artist cannot imagine his art, and cannot perceive it until it is complete.

3. HOW DO VIEWERS RECEIVE THE PAINTING'S MESSAGE?

Ordinary experience of objects seems to raise no problems. The observer opens his eyes and sees his environment; he shuts them and blots out the view. He walks among objects and gains different perspectives of them. He finds that he can touch most objects that are within reach. He talks to others about these objects and shares expectations concerning them. Such common observations convince us that the familiar world of objects has continuity in time and space, which is independent of our scrutiny. The eyes provide specific images of this world; different senses make other properties accessible. Similarly as the artist and his artwork's viewer, in visual science and art each is attempting to communicate mental images through patterns, structures and forms; they also change the object of interest through observation and perception in the qualitative domain of cognition and in the quantitative domain of measurements (M. Johnson [17]). Visual science and art can therefore be regarded each as a mode of communication of mental imagery by pattern or structure in some selected medium. In contrast to the scientist, the artist is absorbed by the shock of the discovery itself. His response to it is to create a form, which will enable his appreciators to make the same discovery or rediscovery of a common pattern among items of experience for themselves. The fundamental way in which the aesthetic object conforms to the subject is by analogy. The subject transforms the object itself by making perceptual, imaginative, emotive and conceptual analogies of the object. In so doing the form, the aesthetic identity of the work of art, is translated to the appreciator. These translations or analogues of the work are the meanings of which it is significant. They exist, however, within the mind of the appreciator and reflect aspects of his self-identity. These meanings constitute the subjective sense of the work's self-significance. The work of art, then, is self-significant in two senses: objective and subjective. Since this relation of the aesthetic object to its meanings within the appreciator is the same as the relation of a natural symbol to its meaning, the aesthetic object is called a self-significant natural symbol.

Aesthetic perception in the visual arts, information science and psychology Neuro–Aesthetics I

"Denotation is the core of representation and is independent of re-resemblance". The semantic domain encompasses those special techniques which delineate and define dimensions such as perspective and equilibrium. These techniques are essentially geometrical, as opposed to expressive" (A. Moles [18])

Aesthetic information includes the expressive organization of physical and sensory aspects of a work of art, which does not serve to denote objects. This category of information is very broad indeed, defining the style of a painting through the selection of particular colors, brush-stroke techniques, or ways of connecting forms.

According to Moles, aesthetic information is (1) specific to the channel transmitting it (e.g., a painting versus a symphony); (2) determines "internal states" including emotions and sensory reactions; (3) is not translatable (e.g., a symphony cannot replace an animated cartoon); and (4) is uniquely personal.

The term, which most closely approximates these ideas, is "syntactic information". Incorporating structuralistic views, A. Moles [18] has elegantly argued that a work of art can simultaneously embody qualitatively independent levels of organization superimposed upon each other. Each level conveys its own unique message and possesses specific rules of organization. The two major levels of organization are the semantic and the aesthetic. Behaviorally oriented aestheticians like Berlyne (Figure 38 [19]) described the spectator as reacting to the work of art. He cites the results from a variety of factor-analytic studies, involving both visual and musical material, which suggests two dimensions of reaction: Uncertainty: simple-complex, and Hedonic Tone: displeasing-pleasing. Uncertainty judgments tend to increase monotonically as a function of the objective complexity of the stimulus.

Hedonic Tone judgments are represented by an inverted U-shaped curve, suggesting an interaction between the properties of the stimulus and an organizational process in the spectator. The observer, rather than merely responding to the aesthetic object at many levels simultaneously, including the sensory, cognitive-intellectual, emotional, conceptualizes these different levels during perception: This confirms the subjective predictions of the viewer/listener (reflecting his training, personal history) in a sensory-motor sequence of eye fixations permitting him the specific "view" that fits his personal capabilities and preferences at this time. The integration of these many levels reflects the meanings of the aesthetic object for the spectator at a particular moment. Thus set, context, and individual differences among spectators may eventuate in very different "reactions" – obviously inter-actions – along the uncertainty factors for the very same aesthetic materials. A non-behaviouristic, cognitive neuro-psychologically and phenomenologically oriented approach maintains that the spectator does not merely react to a work of art but rather interacts with it [20]. The spectator brings to the aesthetic episode skills of visual sensibility needs, moods, feelings, expectations, which shape his examination and experience of the work of art [21]. Dufrenne [22] acknowledges the role of the spectator when he states that the work of art is transformed into an "*aesthetic object*" during the process of aesthetic perception. This reminds us of the basic message of the concept that believes in the creative visual mind and cognition of the spectator as the sole source of "art". Art per se is non-existent, for its material subject is non-art without the spectator [13].

The observer, rather than merely responding to the aesthetic object at many levels simultaneously, including sensory physiological, cognitive-intellectual, emotional levels. conceptualizes these different levels during perception. Confirming his subjective predictions (reflecting his training, personal history etc.) in a sensory-motor sequence of eye fixations permitting him the ever specific "view" that fits his personal capabilities and preferences at this time. The integration of these many levels reflects the meanings of the aesthetic object for the spectator at a particular moment. Thus set, context, and individual differences among spectators may eventuate in very different "reactions" – obviously inter-actions – along the uncertainty factors for the very same aesthetic materials.

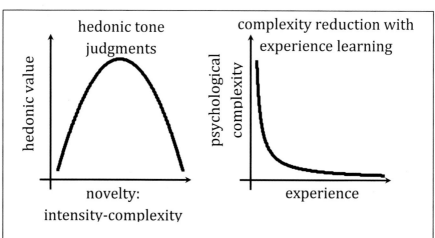

Figure 37. Hedonic Tone judgments are represented by an inverted U-shaped curve, left; physiological complexity and learning, right [23].

The observer, rather than merely responding to the aesthetic object at many levels simultaneously, including sensory physiological, cognitive-intellectual, emotional levels. conceptualizes these different levels during perception. Confirming his subjective predictions (reflecting his training, personal history etc.) in a sensory-motor sequence of eye fixations permitting him the ever specific "view" that fits his personal capabilities and preferences at this time. The integration of these many levels reflects the meanings of the aesthetic object for the spectator at a particular moment. Thus set, context, and individual differences among spectators may eventuate in very different "reactions" – obviously inter-actions – along the uncertainty factors for the very same aesthetic materials.

The material medium of art. The work of art itself comprises an arrangement of material elements such as canvas or wood, oil or acrylic paint, which define its medium and its basic physical qualities. The pattern or configuration of these material elements then determines the structure of the work. Incorporating structuralistic views A. Moles [18] has elegantly argued that a work of art can simultaneously embody qualitatively independent levels of organization superimposed upon each other. Each level conveys its own unique message and possesses specific rules of organization. The two major levels of organization are the semantic and the aesthetic. Goodman [24] offers a simple and clear account of the semantic information, which may be contained within a picture. "The plain fact is that a picture, to represent an object, must be a symbol for it, stand for it, and refer to it." That art is "creation" rather than "imitation" has been noted in various forms from the time of Leonardo, who insisted that the painter is "Lord of all Things", to that of Klee, who wanted to create as Nature does. This more metaphysical notion disappears when we realize that we are surrounded by posters and newspapers carrying illustrations of commodities or events. Differences between the approaches of information theorists – involved in memory research and neuropsychological aestheticians [25], have been noted by Berlyne and others. Information theorists emphasize the practical or instrumental value of perception. Hence, they maintain that the "transient products" of preliminary physical or sensory analyses may be discarded in favor of the results of "deeper" semantic analyses [25]. They also argue (Lockhart, Craik, & Jacoby, 1976) that a person is consciously aware of only that level of analysis, which receives attention and extensive processing. From the perspective of neuropsychological aesthetics, all levels of processing, including sensory and semantic analyses, are of equal importance. Further, the aesthetic set of the spectator sensitizes him to all levels of analysis. These "levels" may be processed simultaneously or in parallel. This implies that the aesthetic set involves a broader mode of attention, which can grasp interactions among the levels.

4. THE RELATION OF VIEWER AND OBJECT

If vision is an active grasp, what does it take hold of? If an observer intently examines an object, she finds her eyes well equipped to see minute detail. Yet, visual perception does not operate with the mechanical faithfulness of a camera, which records everything impartially: the whole set of tiny bits of shape and color constituting the eyes and mouth of the person posing for the photograph, as well as the corner of the telephone protruding accidentally behind his head. What do we see when we see? Seeing means grasping some outstanding features of objects: the blueness of the sky, the curve of the flamingo's neck, the rectangularity of the book, the straightness of the pencil. A few simple lines and dots are readily accepted as "a face," not only by civilized Westerners, who may be suspected of having agreed among one another on such "sign language," but also by babies, savages, and animals. They as we must have some internal model of what-to-look-for. Objects-as-seen were distinguished from objects-in-the-world, when men have formulated theories of their relation. A desire to establish resemblance, structural equivalence, isomorphism, correspondence, or some other mode of correlation between the presumed complementary entities is evident in the writings of commentators since ancient times. This theme runs through the development of the science of geometrical optics. It has been influential in guiding research in the anatomy and physiology of the visual receptors and their projections in the brain, and it remains with us in contemporary formulations of the psychology of perception. Great progress has been made in these several sciences and has influenced formulation of the relation between sensed object and its correlate. Yet new explanations seem always to lead to new dilemmas [26] with the increasing "aesthetic versus content" aspect in pictures and works of art.

5. THE RELATIONSHIP BETWEEN THE AESTHETIC OBJECT AND THE SUBJECT'S MIND

The movement to devaluate the content in favor of the purely aesthetic or pictorial aspect has been with us for a long time in history, at least since the seventeenth century; but also in quite earlier times, obviously without the "consciousness" of the artist living in the evolving "scientific revolution." And therefore, Cubist and Abstract art actually represent further steps in this development. The medieval church and philosophers, such as Scotus Eriugena, held the view that *true beauty belonged to God.* The basic material of arts was believed as the relics and depositories of paganism. The serious philosophical theory of art as play can justly be said to originate with Kant. Distinguishing fine art from handicraft, Kant wrote:

"We regard the first as if it could only prove purposive as play, i.e., as an occupation that is pleasant in itself. But the second is regarded as if it could only be compulsorily imposed upon one as work."

Schiller took up the analogy in both senses of the word "play" gave it a metaphysical flavor and made it central to his aesthetic theory. Generally, three art theories are to be distinguished: Theories arguing from the assumption that art is man's own substitute for reality (Greece, China, India), theories that derive from interest in the functions of art: the conception of art as an instrument for the communication of feeling and emotion, and even expansion of experience, and a third, more modern concept: In the 20th century, we find a new group of formalistic theories, proposing that certain qualities, which are comprised of the term "form", are distinctive of aesthetic value.

In the past there was the History of Art and there was Aesthetics. Up until to the Renaissance, works of art were usually dedicated to God and followed the rules laid down by the Church. It is only with the Renaissance that they ceased to be strictly devotional objects and were appreciated for their own sake. On the other hand, Aesthetics, making the most of the resurrection of the antique philosophers, particularly Plato, started to debate and dogmatize on the goals which the artist should pursue to attempt to define the essence of art, namely beauty. Art and aesthetics were separate domains between which there was no bridge. Modern physics insists on "objects" as, e.g., electrons that we cannot perceive directly with our senses. Similarly, modern art has liberated the artist from the primitive goal of producing a copy of natural objects accessible to sense perception. In painting the choice of objects, color etc. follows a code of imagination flow, which determines the whole setup. In science and art, a conformity exists between the aesthetic or the scientific object and the subject's state of mind, although the channel for information exchange between the artist and his viewer/his audience may be very noisy. There is a convergence of modern art and modern science, especially physics, in that the limits of conceptualization are reached in both fields: compare the imagination of subatomic particles with the minimal change of artful thinking by concept artists as pointed out by D. Ballard [27], and more recently by A. C. Danto [28] (Figure 38: see Two examples of concept art by Astrid Klein and Sol Lewitt). Sol Lewitt said:

> "The conventions of art are altered by works of art. Successful art changes our understanding of the conventions by altering our perceptions. Perception of ideas leads to new ideas. The artist cannot imagine his art, and cannot perceive it until it is complete. One artist may mis-perceive and/or understand it differently than the artist: As a work of art but still be set off in his own chain of thought by that misconstrual. Perception is subjective. The artist may not necessarily understand his own art" (Published in 0-9 (New York), 1969, and Art-Language (England), May 1969)

Studies towards a "modern" conception of the antagonism of art and scientific thought by Pollack (1947) showed that two observations demonstrate a relationship between scientific thought and art: Scientific knowledge requires a universally communicable logical structure, which is also true for the criticism and appreciation of art, only with certain differences in interpretation. The artist constructs between object analogies, or as Whitehead [29] expresses it: "a transference of subjective form from the feeling of one object to that of another."

experience error

Figure 38. Two examples of concept art by Astrid Klein (a, left) and Sol Lewitt.

The artistic venture is a venture in movement. The analogous action, which he woos, may be at the level of perception, imagination, emotion, or even conceptualization. If what one makes are analogies incorporating the pattern of something else in his chosen material, then he is a creative artist. If one merely responds to a work of art organizing conceptual sets, corresponding to the external world then he is an appreciator. In either case there exists a conformity between the aesthetic object and the subject's state of mind. Specifically, this conformity is expressed as a course of analogies at various levels of the work of art. When the movement among these analogies is valued for its own sake, then the subject is undergoing the neuro-aesthetic experience. The course of analogies of science and art at various levels and the movement among these analogies appear to reflect Pollack's understanding that the viewer applies his internal model on the work of art to be considered: finally finding neuro-aesthetic experience and resolution through changing his model's levels while looking. Compared to modern science, the four problems in modern art are: Abstraction. Flattening of the picture plane. The tendency to theorize as a conscious preoccupation with arts about historical accomplishments, particularly with theoretical interpretations of the different movements. And the "perceptual" nature of art with its involvement in what and how we "see", as in "Impressionism". Vitz's thesis [30] suggests that modern art is not interpretable without an understanding of the contributions of modern science, especially of the visual sciences. There is a lack of appreciation of science by historians and critics of modern art, he feels, and they are too formalistic [31]. Written from an art theory perspective "the artist paints in order to see his art", i.e., "with the aesthetic or imaginative experience which is the work of art" [32]. What converts impressions into ideas, or sensation into imagination in the activity of awareness or consciousness? There are no artistic ideas without impressions. Colingwood [32] is, in fact, assuming two different theories of aesthetic experience, one for the artist, another for the audience. For the aesthetic experience in itself, he assumes, is in both cases a purely inward experience, taking place wholly in the mind of the person who enjoys it. He correctly implies two different models with the work of art in between; he reasons incorrectly that only sensualistic bottom-up driven "impressions" drive artistic ideas as well as the viewer's perception of the work of art.

Parker and Deregowski [33] claimed, concerning visual perception and artistic style with contemporary paintings, it is sometimes difficult to tell whether one is confronting a work of art or whether one has inadvertently strayed into the laboratory of a visual art scientist. This view, however simplistic, does enable one to see a thread which has run through artistic endeavour over the last five hundred years. Inevitably the characteristics of the eye have been of concern to visual artists. The most recent one to draw on this theme was David Hockney [5] commenting how the invention of optical techniques almost immediately changed the way how artists looked at space. The thesis that one of the essential features of artistic style consists of the particular characteristics of the eye's mechanisms that the painter chooses to explore is however an idea that had not been extensively examined although it has been implicit in the work of a number of commentators. Again, the "style" implies a new adjustment of the viewer's model onto the work of art, particularly when the artist used new techniques to translate his own model.

Symmetry and its removal – Neuro-Aesthetics II

One of the major principles of compositional design is symmetry. Concerning the approach to study art appreciation and formal art training one must ask, if there is an "abstract utopia" with ideal forms of terrestial representations. Symmetry is one of the techniques used by artists to achieve a pleasing design. However, visual symmetry involves much more than simple balance. A perfectly balanced painting would be rather boring, as would a perfectly balanced building, face, or even personality. While we understand order, we find minor visual dislocations interesting and invest greater effort in investigating them. Some idealistic art scholars maintain that idealized forms exist in a type of abstract utopia and that terrestrial forms are only counterfeit representations, each of which, more or less accurately, resembles the ideal. One measure of the merit of art is its approximation to the ideal. Others, more socially or behaviorally oriented, insist that art appreciation is learned and is based on social and environmental factors. It is generally agreed that art education teaches principles of balance, proportion, and symmetry as powerful forces in pictorial composition, and that artists for centuries – especially

Western artists – have faithfully applied these principles in their work. One of the major principles of compositional design is symmetry. Symmetry is used in art primarily to achieve a balanced design. Balance can be achieved formally by reflectively transforming compositional structures about an axis of symmetry, but perfectly isomorphic compositions are rare in art. Rather, artists more typically use symmetry as a design principle for arranging and weighting pictorial elements of a composition to produce a stable, holistic pattern. The goal of this weighting process is to achieve a sense of perceptual balance and harmony among compositional elements, which may influence the aesthetic judgments of sophisticated viewers because they are better able to relate issues of compositional design and balance to a derived structural skeleton as compared to naive viewers [34]. Nodine and McGinnis [35] have shown that Bouleau-type geometrically defined structures predict which pictorial features of art compositions receive the focus of visual attention as measured by eye fixations. Therefore, the knowledge of structural principles may facilitate the perceptual analysis of art compositions.

Figure 39. Seurat's Les Poseuses showing four of the five areas of compositional content – Center Figure, Fore Figure, Background (BG), and Changed Figure (Back Figure is absent) – used to identify pictorial elements contributing to the geometric symmetry of design.

Seurat's Les Poseuses showing four of the five areas of compositional content – Center Figure, Fore Figure, Background (BG), and Changed Figure (Back Figure is absent) – used to identify pictorial elements contributing to the geometric symmetry of design. The analysis of the breakdown of the composition into content areas is based on Bouleau geometric analysis of Seurat's painting [36]. This identifies the central standing figure and two seated figures "governed by isoscaled triangles" on either side. The final area that is identified is the area containing La Grandejatte, which was shifted to the far left to perturb the balance of the modified version.

REFERENCES

[1]   D. Noton and L. W. Stark, "Scanpaths in eye movements during pattern perception," *Science,*, vol. 171, pp. 308–311, 1971.

[2]   D. Noton and L. W. Stark, "Scanpaths in saccadic eye movements while viewing and recognizing patterns," *Vis. Res.*, vol. 11, pp. 929–942, 1971.

[3]   S. Martinez-Conde, J. Otero-millan, and S. L. Macknik, "The impact of microsaccades on," *Nat. Rev. Neurosci.*, vol. 14, no. 2, pp. 83–96, 2013.

[4]   C. M. Privitera, T. Carney, S. Klein, and M. Aguilar, "Analysis of microsaccades and pupil dilation reveals a common decisional origin during visual search," *Vision Res.*, vol. 95, pp. 43–50, 2014.

[5]   Lawrence Weschler, "The looking glass: The Modern master David Hockney has a theory"," *New Yorker*, vol. January 31, pp. 65–75, 2000.

[6]   S. Zeki, "Artistic creativity and the brain.," *Science,*, vol. 293, p. 51–52., 2001.

[7]   E. H. H. Gombrich, "How to read a painting," in *Series of the "Saturday EveningPost" "Adventures of the Mind,"* New York: Knopf, 1961.

[8]   E. D. Gombrich EH, *Looking for answers. Conversations on art and science.* New York: Abrams Publ., 1993.

[9]   R. Arnheim, *Art and Visual Perception*. Berkeley.: University of California Press, 1951.

[10] C. Shannon and W. Weaver, *A mathematical theory of communication*. Urbana Illinois: University of Illinois Press., 1949.

[11] W. H. Zangemeister and L. Stark, *The Artistic Brain Beyond the Eye*. 2007.

[12] W. H. Zangemeister and C. M. Privitera, "Parsing eye movement analysis of scanpaths of naïve viewers of art: How do we differentiate art from non-art pictures?," *J. Eye Mov. Reseach*, vol. 6, no. 2, pp. 1–33, 2013.

[13] M. Duchamp, "Apropos of 'Readymades'.," in *Duchamp: A biography.*, C. Tomkins, Ed. New York: Henry Holt, 1921.

[14] Schalkwijk J. P. M. and T. Kailath, ""A coding scheme for a Co, dditive noise channels with feedback part I: No bandwidth restraint(I) and(II) "A coding scheme for additive noise Signals, channels with feedback part II: Band-limited," *IEEE Trans. Info. Theory*, vol. 12, pp. 172–182, 1966.

[15] A. Sillito and K. Grieve, "A re-appraisal of the role of layer VI of the visual cortex in the generation of cortical end inhibition.," *Exp. Brain Res.*, vol. 87, pp. 521–529, 1991.

[16] M. Bense, *Aesthetica*. Baden-Baden: Agis Verlag, 1965.

[17] M. Johnson, *Art and scientific thought; towards a modern revision of their antagonism,*. London,: Faber and Faber, 1944.

[18] Moles A, *Information theory and aesthetic perception,*. Urbana, Univ. of Illinois Press, 1966.

[19] D. E. Berlyne, *Aesthetics and psychobiology*. New York: Appleton-Century- Crofts, 1971.

[20] W. H. Zangemeister, K. Sherman, and L. W. Stark, "Evidence for a global scanpath strategy in viewing abstract compared with realistic images," *Neuropsychologia*, vol. 33, no. 8, pp. 1009–1025, 1995.

[21] M. Hester, "Are Paintings and Photographs Inherently Interpretative?," *J. Aesthet. Art Crit.*, vol. 31:, p. 235–46., 1972.

[22] M. Dufrenne, *The phenomenology of aesthetic perception*. Evenston: M. N. Western Univ. Press, 1973.

[23] D. E. J. Berlyne, "The influence of complexity and novelty in visual figures on orienting responses," *Exp. Psychol.*, vol. 55, no. 296, pp. 289–296, 1958.

[24] Goodman N., *Languages of art: An Approach to a theory of symbols.* Indianapolis: The Bobbs-Merrill Company, 1968.

[25] F. I. M. Craik and R. S. Lockhart, "Levels of processing: A framework of memory research," *J. verbal Learn. verbal beahaviour*, vol. 2, pp. 671–684, 1972.

[26] K. G. G., *Structure in art and in science.* New York: Braziller, 1974.

[27] E. G. Ballard, "Art and analysis - an essay toward a theory in aesthetics," *J. Philos.*, vol. 58, pp. 137–140, 1961.

[28] A. Danto, *The philosophical disenfranchisement of art.* New York: Columbia University Press, 1986.

[29] R. Deleuze, "Whitehead and the transformation of metaphysics," in *Royal Academy of Art (Transl.)*, C. A. and R. K. Eds., Ed. Brussels, 2005, pp. 7–19.

[30] P. C. Vitz and A. Glimche, *Modern art and modern science : the parallel analysis of vision.* New York: Praeger, 1984.

[31] C. Bell, *Art.* New York: Putnam, 1914.

[32] Colingwood R. G., *The Principles of art.* Oxford: Clarendon, 1978.

[33] D. K. Parker and J. B. Deregowski, "Perception and artistic style," in *Advances in Psychology - 73*, Amsterdam New York: North-Holland, Elsevier, 1990, p. 175.

[34] D. Marschalek and F. Neperud, "The National Gallery of Art Laserdisk and accompanying database: A means to enhance art instruction.," *Art Educ.*, vol. 44, no. 3, pp. 48–53, 1983.

[35] C. F. Nodine and J. J. Mcginnis, "Artistic Style, compositional design and visual Scanning," *Vis. Arts Res.*, vol. 9, no. 1, pp. 1–9, 1993.

[36] P. Locher and C. Nodine, "The perceptual value of symmetry," *Comput. Math. with Appl.*, vol. 17, no. 4–6, pp. 475–484, 1989.

Chapter 4

WHEN EVERYTHING COULD BE ART AND EVERYBODY COULD BE AN ARTIST, THEN WHAT IS ART CRITIQUE?

The mode of viewing artful pictures versus snapshots can be distinguished by expectation and training; when these are sophisticated, we find differences in viewing modes. With minor training and expectation this stays on a low level, and we find no differences of viewing modes. This is due to the global invariant components of eye movements that are connected in the viewer's brain to different, often historical views of art, – if anything at all. Therefore art-viewing may be dissipating and sometimes arbitrary in spite of the basic facts of perception and training. So, in our post-postmodern times of global art world art critic could be pointless. However, art criteria may be still relevant and are used in a world where superfluous information deluges not only visual art, its creation and critic.

1. VIEWING ARTFUL PICTURES VERSUS NON-ART SNAPSHOTS

Let us recall some useful facts from the preceding chapters. That art is "creation" rather than "imitation" has been noted from the time of Leonardo, who insisted that the painter is "Lord of all Things", to that of Klee, who wanted to create as Nature does. This more metaphysical notion disappears when we realize that posters and newspapers carrying illustrations of commodities or events surround us. This leads to some subconscious ambiguity of the sceneries in pictures that surround us and may puzzle, surprise and please us. Top-down knowledge is divided into two: General knowledge – all we know or think we know, which includes abstract concepts far beyond perception; and perceptual knowledge which is limited to what is needed for reading bottom-up signals from the eyes and other senses. "So we can have an illusion, and know it is an illusion" (R. Gregory [1]).

As a third dimension for vision the task for which vision should be working as appropriately as possible is, of course, consciousness. The store of knowledge for perception is shown as smaller and separate from general conceptual knowledge, for there is strong evidence that perception cannot tap all our conceptual knowledge and understanding. As the examination of the object proceeds, all levels can simultaneously contribute to the aesthetic experience. The "stages" of perception may simply be components of aesthetic perception, with little inherent organizational quality. Thus, what the viewer has to do is take the components of the sequential, stage-oriented approach and restructure them in such a way as to allow for the plasticity of perception, change over time, and the concept of meaning as a holistic, context-bound process.

2. VIEWS AND DEFINITIONS OF ART:
CLASSICAL AND MODERN VIEWS

Aristotle was the first to introduce the theory that art imitates nature (*mimesis*) and attributed the origin of art to the human affinity for imitation. Based on mimesis he distinguished three classes of art: 1st, difference in the means of imitation: rhythm, language, harmony relating to music, poetry, dance and drama; 2nd the examination of the object being represented; 3rd the manner in which the object is presented. Hence, art is a productive science: It is found within the object produced, not within the mind of the artist, and this determines the quality of the art. The viewer (evaluator) of the piece of art does not need to consider the message or intent of the artist or the history or circumstances behind the work when evaluating it critically: Even if the message of the artist may be absent or unclear, the object itself may be a perfect imitation and therefore a perfect piece of art. Aristotle's theory of art as imitation in this way provides a basis for classification of art forms. His theory appeals to human nature – especially in view of the more recent findings on mirror neurons in the human cortex and their variant functions (Rizzolatti [2]) – but it lacks more refined ideas about the creativity of the artist, about the viewer's response and about abstract art forms. Immanuel Kant and G. W. F. Hegel ascribed far greater importance to natural rather than to artistic beauty, so far as there were grounds for distinguishing them: for them the assurance of a deep intended harmony between the world and us.

Marcel Duchamp has changed this view radically: "Art is a drug: Art has absolutely no existence as veracity, as truth. The onlooker is important as the artist" [3]. According to Duchamp, in the creative act, the artist goes from intention to realization through a chain of totally subjective reactions. His struggle toward the realization is a series of efforts, pains, satisfactions, refusals, decisions, which also cannot and must not be fully self-conscious, at least on the aesthetic plane. The result of this struggle is a difference between the intention and its realization, a difference which the artist is not aware of: It is like an arithmetical relation between the unexpressed but intended and the unintentionally expressed. The creative act takes another aspect when the spectator experiences the phenomenon of transmutation: through the change from inert matter into a work of art in the mind's eye of the viewer who determines the weight of the work of art on an aesthetic scale. The spectator brings the work in contact with the external world by deciphering and interpreting its inner qualifications and thus adds his contribution to the creative act. Recent studies show that as an active top down process, vision and higher order cognitive influences such as memory retrieval and expectation, attention, perceptual task as well as motor signals are fed into the sensory apparatus [4]. Duchamp's view has had a major influence on art of the 20th century in many respects that are beyond the scope of the present considerations.

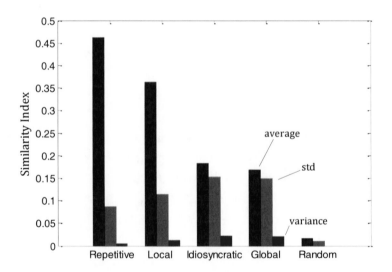

Figure 40. Similarity of sequences of repetitive (R), local (L, specific local parts of a picture), idiosyncratic (I, the special characteristic of a particular viewer) and global (G) viewing conditions. Note the high similarity index for R and L as expected from previous findings; also note the low similarity index for I and R that is in the range of the standard deviation; blue column: average similarity value; red column: standard deviation; dark red column: variance.

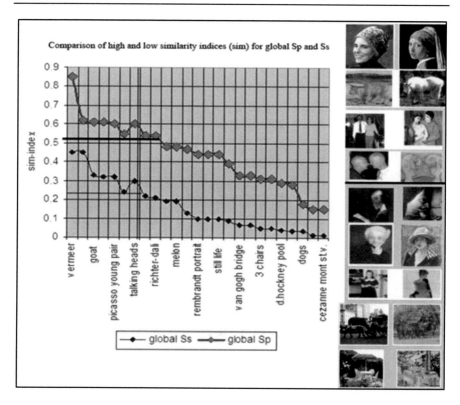

Figure 41. Similarity indices examples of nine picture pairs (right) for sequential averaged global responses out of 25 pairs. Sp is similarity of eye positions, i.e., fixations; Ss is similarity of eye sequences.

The other major influence and also departure from traditional art is represented by the work of Andy Warhol and his lasting influence on Pop Art and its followers. Alluding to the pure and perfect surface of things he said:

"There I am. There's nothing behind it. I see everything that way, the surface of things, a kind of mental Braille. I just pass my hands over the surface of things. The reason I'm painting this way is that I want to be a machine, and I feel that whatever I do and do machine-like is what I want to do. I like boring things. I like things to be exactly the same over and over again" [5].

The postmodern art philosopher Arthur Danto [6] extended this to:

> "Natural beauty is always external; when we see the world itself as a
> work of art, and its significance as the symbol of their kindness."

In a recent study (Zangemeister and Privitera [7]) we asked, do naïve subjects perceive a snapshot in a different manner than they perceive an artful picture; or is there no difference in perception and thus a high similarity between the spatial and sequential scanpath regions of interests. And further: Is the global similarity during scanning of all image-pairs in all subjects low, i.e., close to random, or is there a high similarity of scanpaths when artful pictures were viewed, but not in viewing snapshots? As a result, there was no basic difference between viewing artful pictures or snapshots within our somewhat naïve group, as far as viewing "art" was concerned. Using high resolution infrared eye recordings in 7 young naïve subjects we recorded their scanpaths of 4 sec viewing 50 pairs of 25 artful pictures and 25 snapshot photographs on 5 different days. The pictures were selected with respect to similarity of size and scene between the snapshots and the artful pictures.

After string editing and parsing analysis [7, 8, 9] we compared the *repetitive* [subjects viewed picture several times in a row] and the *global* [subjects viewed picture one time with task to recognize the general, "global" layout of picture] similarity indices. Normalized similarity indices [how similar eye movements where in both situations], similarity of eye movement positions, i.e., fixations, and similarity of eye movement sequences were compared. Even without any specific task instruction for general viewing conditions when different subjects look at the same picture, they are fairly consistent in identifying regions of interest as indicated in this study by high local (L) and high repetitive (R) values. The strong scanpath consistency reported in human experiments when no specific objective is given to the subjects means that only a specific restricted set of representative regions in the internal cognitive model of the picture is essential for the brain to perceive and eventually recognize the picture. This representative set is quite similar for different, in our case art-naïve subjects and different picture pairs independently of their art – non art features.

For 21 pairs of paintings and snapshots subjects either did not show any viewing similarities, i.e., similarity index close to 0.11; or they did show some higher viewing similarities between snapshots and artful pictures, such that their EM scanpaths demonstrated similarity indices that somewhat differed from random (non significantly). Only in 4 out of the 25 artful-picture snapshot pairs (16%) was a higher similarity value found. This indicates that only a comparatively small proportion of our subjects may have been aware of the artfulness of some pictures. This was corroborated by our post-test question to quickly select possible artful pictures (14% on average) within pairs.

3. GLOBAL INVARIANT COMPONENTS OF EYE MOVEMENTS

Global-invariant components of eye movements – the use of some global eye movement strategy control – is highest in reading, i.e., start at the upper left, proceed horizontally and downwards. "Reading artful pictures" (Gombrich [10, 11]), is a similarly difficult and only with long term training achievable skill.

Global-invariant components of eye movements may generally be small. However, with skillful internal models as in *reading* sentences or artful pictures we might expect significantly different global similarity indices from the repetitive and local conditions. Degree of information (top down), and particularity (bottom-up) in our paradigm were shown to be intimately interconnected. Thus, differential viewing of art pictures compared to snapshots rarely showed up in our naïve subjects. Obviously, the knowing viewer must apply a pre-existent top down sophisticated model of "artfulness" in a particular picture, in order to differentiate it from a simple snapshot that looks similar. Overall, one could divide viewers into three subgroups with respect to the capability of distinguishing art: Naïve (almost no differentiation) to sophisticated (capable to differentiate art – non art in traditional aesthetics), to the modern and postmodern professional viewer (capable to distinguish any piece of work, including a "ready- made" as art from non-art).

The antithesis of modernist art was kitsch

The antithesis of modernist art was kitsch: C. Greenberg made this dialectic the subject of his first article on all "Avant-Garde and Kitsch," published in 1939 [12], and he never changed his mind:

"Kitsch at its lowest was popular, commercial art and literature with their chromeotypes, magazine covers, illustrations, ads, slick and pulp fiction, comics, Tin Pan Alley music, tap dancing, Hollywood movies, etc., etc. Low art was bad enough, but even worse was a more "elevated" brand of kitsch, which displayed the trappings of high art without challenging received ideas or taste. In the struggle between authentic high culture and debased popular culture, there could be no compromise. In order to avoid contamination by kitsch. High art had to withdraw into its own area of competence and into abstraction. "[13]

Or, as H. Rosenberg observed [14]:

"Materials that are more real, or actual, than others-for example, brown dirt rather than brown paint-imply a decision to purge art of the seeds of artifice. Digging holes or trenches in the ground, cutting tracks through a cornfield, laying a square sheet of lead in the snow (the so-called earthworks art) do not in their de-aestheticizing essence differ in any way from exhibiting a pile of mail sacks, tacking a row of newspapers on a wall, or keeping the shutter of a camera open while speeding through the night (the so-called anti-form art)... Aesthetic withdrawal also paved the way for "process" art, in which biological, physical, or seasonal forces affect the original materials and either change their form or destroy them, as in works incorporating growing grass and bacteria or inviting rust-and random art, whose form and content are decided by chance. Ultimately, the repudiation of the aesthetic suggests the total elimination of the art object and its replacement by an idea for a work or by the rumor that one has been consummated- as in conceptual art."

Despite the stress on the actuality of the materials used, the principle common to all classes of de-aestheticized art was that the finished product, if any, was of less significance than the procedures that brought the work into being and of which it is the trace. The movement toward de-aestheticization was both a reaction against and a continuation of the trend toward formalistic over-refinement in the art of the sixties, and particularly in the rhetoric that accompanied it. "The current defiance of the aesthetic is the latest incident in the perennial reversion to primitivism in the art of the past hundred years and the exaltation of ruggedness, simplicity, and doing what one chooses without regard to the public and its representatives. On the other hand, de-aestheticized art is the latest of the avant-garde movements, and is presently engaged in permeating and taking over leadership in the situation it symbolically denounces" [14].

"To distinguish modernism from postmodernism..." literary theorist Ihab Hassan [15] drew up lists of opposing terms that would serve equally well in distinguishing minimalism from post-minimalism. Among the terms were:

The dialectics of modern and post-modern art

Modernism	Postmodernism
Form (conjunctive/closed)	Antiform (disjunctive/open)
Design	Chance
Art Object/Finished Work	Process/Performance/Happening
Creation/Totalization	Decreation/Deconstruction
Centering	Dispersal
Selection	Combination

The post-minimalists embraced Freud's idea of theatricality. So, did artists in succeeding movements and their supporters, often using it as the point of departure in their discourse. For example, art theorist Douglas Crimp, in an update on a seminal show titled Pictures he had curated in 1977, remarked that the work of the artists included, which incorporated "photographs, film, video, performance, as well as traditional modes of painting, drawing, and sculpture," had been deliberately theatrical in that it was preoccupied with time, or, as Freud had written, "with the duration of experience". Crimp also wrote:

"Freud's fears were well founded. For if temporality was implicit in the way minimal sculpture was experienced, then it would be made thoroughly explicit – in fact the only possible manner of experience – for much of the art that followed" [13].

4. AESTHETICS OF ART VERSUS NON-ART: IF ANYTHING CAN BE ART, IS ART CRITICISM THEN SUPERFLUOUS?

Since then, definitions of art are abundant, and there is no clear consensus more about "What is art?" Some artists such as Ben Vautier announced at the Documenta 1972 "everything is art", – reminiscent of aul Feyerabend's statement from 1964: "Anything Goes" that alludes to his epistemological anarchism. So it seems natural to ask polemically with Tsion Avital: "Is modern art about art?" He argues that modern art is in a state of utter confusion. To distinguish between a state of art, pseudo-art and the inability of many to distinguish between these two extremes [16]. Art critic A. Danto emphasizes, however, that:

"in an age of pluralism in art, when anything might be a work of art (though not everything is), we need a pluralistic critic, willing to see anything as art" [6, 17].

Art criticism generates a surplus of experience and power of judgement in aesthetic discussion. Its engagement with art always begins with the contemplation of the works itself and ends where sensuality is still open to criticism. Critics and artists have in common that both their professions belong to a precarious urban middle class and understand themselves as antipodes to a purposely rationally designed world, meaning the uncertain precarious working and living conditions. In context of the creative class precarious means at the same time an unsafe action that does not result from the outset foreseeable result, or a solid product but in uncertainty. The performance of art and criticism is always precarious because it is dependent on effects and affects, generated in readership and audience. The art critic is concerned with the triad of artist – work – audience; or respectively of curators – exhibition – audience. He produces an inter-active interplay of mediation and translation. As a multiplier he claims the determination of sovereignty over the validity of art and artists.

The experience of art cannot be displayed as a static value, but must be understood as a kind of "dialogue generator" and inspiration for a reshaping process, with the necessary space for experiments and visions, whereby art critics initiate the exchange of insights and discussions. As a counterpart to artistic creation, it has the potential to stimulate on her part new artistic processes. Unfortunately this aspect leads many critics to a characteristically exaggerated opinion of themselves:

> "As an educator, he has a dual function: He leads to the perfection of the art work by congenial linguistic posterior creation and generates a differential expression of a poetic, literary and reflexive innovative text figure" [18].

This sounds like the frequently obtained self-overestimation of the critic, who translates the work of art to the audience and the artist (!) such that he – the critic – is just as creative as the artist. However, the critic's work cannot be regarded as creative as that of an artist, but is best described with service to the arts, which takes place in a distant area. That critics put themselves in public scene at the expense of the event to be described is obviously an issue. Critics may write reviews not about the art, but for the sake of the critic, including their self-promotion, increasing their market value that is owed to the addiction of self-profiling. In the context of a psychological interpretation one might say that in this case the critic gives up the position of the servant, in favor of a claim to power. Critics should have the potential to furnish the reader who has missed an exhibition with insights and knowledge in order to strengthen their own share of a judgment. So he could interact with the artists and museum professionals on to the art system. Unfortunately, this is frequently not the case. Art critics live in the permanent contradiction to make assessments that take more than just subjective validity without an external legitimacy. Art criticism interacts with the claim of public importance: However, it is exercised by persons who empower to this criticism by their profession itself. Out of this dilemma leads something that has to achieve modern art by itself: Art gets legitimized by its results. If one looks at the rise and career of Andy Warhol one discovers the ambivalent behavior of art criticism to Pop Art: Some critics pointed to the affirmative, others to the subversive nature of Warhol's work.

5. DEATH OF CRITICISM?

For several years, the death of art criticism has been lamented in many places. The autopsy of the alleged corpse leads initially to two complementary diagnoses: Strangulation and poisoning. First, strangulation by the market. Death was due to competition from other actors who have power and money on their side. The critics have been displaced by the galleries, the museum organizers, the auction houses and not least the collectors, who accounted for one another, what is to be considered good and high quality. The criticism has done its duty, the critic can disappear. In this picture the critic is good at best as senile, underpaid supplier of adulation and occasional hints of sham culture of debate. But business bohemians do not need any more underpaid complainers. Second, poisoning by modernity. In this reading, the art got rid of its critics. Again, here the critics are compliant: Basically, they become redundant high priests or backers. Their reason and their aesthetic judgment was poisoned insidiously by becoming mystifying phony art charlatans of modernity. Their task is now to talk up their stuff with pseudo-scientific and pseudo-poetic effusions in catalogues, press releases, newspapers and magazines shaking their intimidated audience. This implies of course, that modern and contemporary art requires such a huge deception at all. The death of art critique is merely an inevitable consequence of the atrophy of the art itself, which was robbed of its genuine cognition and aesthetic potency calculated by abstraction, concept, minimal art, etc., – and that can conceal this only with the help of the above mentioned priests and backers. If the diagnosis is that "the art got rid of criticism" then rather the opposite should be considered: It's not the art that got rid of the criticism, but a significant part of the criticism has got ridden of art. That is, a certain portion of the criticism manages in large part to be written without a concrete examination of the works of art themselves. This applies to the portion of critics who mainly see their role in the unmasking of ideological delusions and of artistic false starts; and it applies to those who project themselves primarily as an enthusiastic promoter and supporter of art practice. The late E. Gombrich noted:

"If you take the writings of my colleagues, particularly the critics or art historians, many of the things they say are untranslatable [i.e., untranslatable to scientific language], they are metaphors, like poetry, nothing but emotion. Let me use a figure of speech drawn from banking. The old banknotes always carried the promise that you could exchange them for gold. So with our statements, we ought always to be able to go to the bank and say: give me a fact for it. Therefore I am not very interested in aesthetics or in art criticism, because so much of what these people write is just an expression of their own emotions" [19].

Danto and postmodernism

That all images should be "read" as referring to some imaginary or actual reality appears rather difficult in this context. The painter has to paint "what he sees" because he "knows" it, i.e., his conceptual image. It has been said "that all pictures owe more to other pictures than they do to nature". This is well known in pictorial tradition but contrary to the belief of many artists; the "innocent eye", which should see the world afresh would not see it at all. The conventional vocabulary of basic forms is still indispensable to the artist as a starting point, as a focus of organization.

Rudolf Arnheim has put forward another approach to explain seeing an image:

"I see an object. I see the world around me. What do these statements imply? For the purposes of everyday life, seeing is essentially a means of practical orientation, of determining with one's eyes that a certain thing is present at a certain place and that it is doing a certain thing. This is identification at its bare minimum. A man entering his bedroom at night may perceive a dark patch on the white pillow and thus "see" that his wife is in the familiar place. Under better lighting conditions he will see more, but in principle orientation in a familiar setting requires only a minimum of cues.

Patients suffering from visual agnosia due to brain damage might not recognize even such basic shapes as a circle or a triangle. In getting along in daily life: How would they manage in the street?" On the sidewalk all things are slim – those are people; in the middle of the street, everything is very noisy, bulky, tall – that can be busses, cars" [20].

The American Pre-Raphaelites, who thought of their art in political and even moral terms, were polemically engaged with the National Academy, which disregarded visual truth in favor of pictorial artifice (Danto [21]). Clement Greenberg, the Nation's number one art critic from 1942 until he resigned over a political disagreement in 1949, entertained a no-less-exalted hope for the avant-garde art of his time. He believed that it fortified the mind against kitsch, which he regarded as the favored aesthetic of totalitarianism. Much of what Greenberg dismissed as kitsch was redeemed as pop art by my immediate predecessor, Lawrence Alloway, who invented the term. Hollywood movies, popular music, pulp fiction, Alloway believed, can sustain the same critical examination as high art. "I do not think I would have written a word about art had it not been for pop. But I wrote about it initially as a philosopher, long before art criticism became a possibility for me." ... The art of the 1970s was produced by the young for the young, who used to whatever degree they could the intoxicating obscurities of intellectual imports from abroad: Derrida, Foucault, Lacan, and the French feminists. The decade of the seventies was something like the Dark Ages, in which hidden forces were working to make a new world without anyone realizing that this process was taking place. The new art world was somewhat despairingly characterized in Theodore Adorno's 1969 work Aesthetic Theory:

> "It is self-evident that nothing concerning art is self-evident any more, not its inner life, not its relation to the world, not even its right to exist. The role of art criticism for this world still remains to be identified" [21].

This later led Danto to advance a rudimentary definition of art: Something is an artwork if it embodies a meaning – the supermarket Brillo box is commercial art that proclaims and celebrates the virtues of its contents, namely soap pads. "Warhol's Brillo Box looks just like this carton, but it is not about Brillo. It is perhaps about commercial art, or what Brillo itself means. So the two objects, outwardly similar, call for different art criticisms. To work through these criticisms, one has to find out what the objects mean and begin from there. Art could look anyway at all. There were no constraints on what artists could do, so far as art was concerned." "A painting must be a feast for the eyes," Delacroix said in his Journal, "but that does not mean that there is no place for reason." Danto extended this statement:

> "Contemporary art is rarely a feast for the eyes. It takes reasoning to bring it into being, and to explain what we are seeing. This does not rule out being bowled over by what one sees; but I don't believe that should be the test of good art. Mostly, a work of art releases its meanings and its methods slowly, rarely all at once.
>
> Someone might say I have ideologized a form of pluralism, one which puts aesthetic preferences out of play. My response is that I regard pluralism as the objective structure of contemporary art history, in which nothing is justifiably preferable to anything else, at least so far as modes of artist production are concerned. That is equivalent to saying there is no objective direction for art to take. This does not rule out distinctions in quality, but only the tendency to believe that quality derives from the genre one supports, for example, visual truth or abstraction or minimalism.
>
> Painting, in part for political reasons, has been somewhat marginalized since the 1970s, but it would be inconsistent with pluralism to lead the cheering section for painting, though in my heart of aesthetic hearts, it is painting that moves me most powerfully.

Pluralism is a consequence of a philosophy of art history, and, if I am right, of where we now are in terms of that history. I must some time discover why art criticism generally is so savagely aggressive against its target, almost, as Chekhov once wrote, as if the writer or artist had committed some terrible crime" [21].

6. WAIVER OF ART CRITERIA OR NOT?

If anything can be art, or at least may be in a new context a la Marcel Duchamp, then this suggests the waiver of criteria of art evaluation. This raises the question whether there can ever be *universal, permanently applicable normative criteria* of art's critical assessment. With respect to science and art and their interrelations Werner Heisenberg has remarked that:

> "The artist tries in his factory to make certain shapes of the world that are themselves regardless of their time understandable; in this he is led to the forms and styles that constitute his works. Science and art form in the course of centuries a human language in which we can talk about the more remote parts of reality. Therefore, the two processes in science and art are not too different."

The problem is: The interesting contemporary art may often mislead those who cannot resist the temptation to codify normatively works of art. For this, we need to put together a toolkit with which we approach this art machinery. A tool box, no mandatory fibula and no instructions manual. It is here, therefore, at this point not possible to enumerate in detail the possible tools and use them as a treatment provider. The criteria of art criticism are always subject to continuous social negotiation. Perhaps, - but we can formulate five basic questions that remain valid as guiding principles: (i) Does the artwork reflect its time? (ii) Does the artist apply the material in a skillful, intelligent and imaginative way? (iii) Is the resulting work of art describably original, funny or witty? (iv) Does this work of art touch or surprise me, – do I learn something new? (v) When I compare the artwork to the allegations contained in it or accompanying it, does it keep this comparison? These questions may offer a way to evaluate a work of art. But to this rating one has to get by oneself. Especially the critic must be willing to stand up for his review, and if necessary to fight.

REFERENCES

[1]   R. L. Gregory, *Even Odder Perceptions*. Routledge, 1994.

[2]   G. Rizzolatti and L. Craighero, "The mirror-neuron system," *Annu. Rev. Neurosci.*, vol. 27, pp. 169–192, 2004.

[3]   M. Duchamp, "Apropos of 'Readymades'.," in *Duchamp: A biography.*, C. Tomkins, Ed. New York: Henry Holt, 1921.

[4]   C. D. Gilbert and W. Li, "Top-down influences on visual processing," *Nat. Rev. Neurosci.*, vol. 14, no. 5, p. 350–363, 2013.

[5]   A. Warhol, *The philosophy of Andy Warhol, From A to B and back again*. New York: Barnes & Noble, 1975.

[6]   A. C. Danto, *Embodied meanings: critical essays and aesthetic meditations*. New York: Farrar, Straus, Giroux, 1994.

[7]   W. H. Zangemeister and C. M. Privitera, "Parsing eye movement analysis of scanpaths of naïve viewers of art: How do we differentiate art from non-art pictures?," *J. Eye Mov. Reseach*, vol. 6, no. 2, pp. 1–33, 2013.

[8]   L. W. Stark, C. M. Privitera, H. Yang, M. Azzariti, Y. F. Ho, T. Blackmon, and D. Chernyak, "Representation of human vision in the brain: How does human perception recognize images?," *J. Electron. Imaging*, vol. 10, no. 1, p. 123, 2001.

[9]   C. M. Privitera and L. W. Stark, "Evaluating image processing algorithms that predict regions of interest," *Pattern Recognit. Lett.*, vol. 19, p. 1037–1043., 1998.

[10] E. H. Gombrich, *The essential Gombrich : selected writings on art and culture by Richard Woodfield*. Phaidon Press London, 1969.

[11] E. H. Gombrich, *Art and Illusion: A Study in the psychology of pictorial representation*. London: Phaidon Press, 1977.

[12] C. Greenberg, "Avant-Garde and Kitsch," in *Greenberg, C. Art and Culture: Critical Essays*, Boston: Beacon press, 1961.

[13] I. Sandler and O. Greenberg, "Art from the late 1960s to the early 1990s," in *Art of the Postmodern Era*, I. Sandler, Ed. New York: Icon Editions, Harper & Collins N.Y., 1996, pp. 332–375.

[14] H. Rosenberg, *The de-definition of art*. Chicago London: Univ Chicago Press, 1972.

[15] I. Hassan, *The Postmodern Turn: Essays in Postmodern Theory and Culture*. Columbus, OH: Ohio State University Press, 1987.

[16] T. Avital, *Art versus nonart: Art out of mind*. Cambridge: Cambridge University Press, 2003.

[17] A. C. Danto, *The abuse of beauty*. Chicago: Open Court Publications, 2003.

[18] Rauterberg H, *Und das ist Kunst?! Eine Qualitätsprüfung*. Frankfurt am. Main: S. Fischer, 2007.

[19] E. H. Gombrich and D. Eribon, *Looking for answers. Conversations on art and science*. New York: Abrams Publ., 1993.

[20] R. Arnheim, *Art and Visual Perception*. Berkeley: University of California Press, 1971.

[21] A. Danto, *From philosophy to art criticism, Commentary of American criticism in a new century*. Berkeley, 1996.

Chapter 5

WHY DO WE LOVE PICTURES
AS WE LOVE NOVELS?

Several people with different perceptual samplings will forever have difficulty communicate about it. But in a larger sense as we read – read the picture – there are two perceptual and imagined worlds, the writer's/artist's and the reader's/viewer's that are reaching out to communicate. The text itself is a coded message accessible only to the privileged sender and receiver. The lower levels of the artifact, the words and their semantics, the sentences and their syntaxes, the paragraphs and their frames for an event, appear to be similarly available to several readers. Yet each of us can paraphrase or interpret uniquely much as we do in the so-called "real" world.

1. VIRTUAL-REALITY WORKS
BECAUSE REALITY IS VIRTUAL

The nature of reality may be an illusion, neither proven nor disproven, and use of technological displays and movement translations provide for the appearance of reality. To understand reality, which is also art and science, we need models. Epistemology, or the theory of knowledge, is based on models. Model making forms knowledge that then can be tested. One could "see models everywhere" – with many levels of models from metaphorical and verbal, to mathematical, homeomorphic and simulated models. New models are constructed by analogic reasoning or propositional construction and may be embedded in brains by evolution of neural structures. Yet they cannot be constructed from external experience. Science and Art is model making. Testing models can be done in two ways. (i) Testing of predictions, which is a form of pragmatism, (ii) Testing of the aesthetic nature of the model, its elegance, its ability to encompass a wide range of phenomena with a uniform and minimal set of structures. Beauty and compactness serve both tested functions. Kuhn, as a historian of science, has described the "paradigm shifts" and the resultant pragmatic efficacy of "normal science" in this respect.

2. THE REPRESENTATION OF KNOWLEDGE IN THE BRAIN

Representation of knowledge in the brain is a big point of discussion. If we follow S. Zeki's statement [1] that the visual mechanisms of the brain are designed to obtain knowledge about the world, we could argue that the world may be the world "out there", but as well our inner world, the brain of the knowledge seeking artist and viewer.

If the function of artistic creativity in art is the same as in science, to obtain knowledge about the world, artists use the same methods of exploration and discovery as science. Zeki chooses examples in abstract art to show how art exposes the various mechanisms of the visual brain – receptive fields, cortical modules, orientation selective cells – like in Mondrian's and B. Newman's work the straight line, or in kinetic art A. Calder and J. Tinguely whose works emphasized different aspect of the motion center of the brain (V5), or with the advent of analytical cubism through P. Picasso and G. Braque the emphasis of non-exact boundaries for color and contrast by eliminating the singularity of the point of view, distance and lighting conditions. However, knowledge cannot be obtained from sensory signals, but only by internal processes, – propositional construction or analogic reasoning – inside the brain as I. Kant pointed out. The internal knowledge clusters, cognitive – spatial models, can then be checked against their success in matching incoming sensory signals via the mechanisms of top down and bottom-up vision – cortical modules and receptive fields. The general schema that has been originally proposed by R. Gregory in 1994 (Figure 42) shows a speculative mind-design for vision. Bottom-up signals from the eye, and other senses are processed physiologically and interpreted or "read" cognitively by object knowledge (top down) and by general rules (sideways). The general rules – such as perspective and Gestalt laws of organization – are syntax; the object knowledge is implicit semantics. Feedback from the successes and failures of an action serve to correct and develop knowledge – hence the importance of hands-on learning. It is suggested that real-time sensory signals flag the present – conceivably with qualia of sensation.

The question of representation in art follows – in our view – the interpretation of the Kantian position, that knowledge can only be obtained internally, and that external signals from the external world only act to correct, check, and stimulate further constructions of internal knowledge. In our view, the function of art is to formulate optional models for the creation in the viewer's mind of "essential or crucial" models: to inspire "AWE" and thus aid in construction of and memory for cognitive-spatial models. S. Hustvedt described that moment as: "A painting creates an illusion of an eternal present, a place where my eyes can rest as if the clock has magically stopped ticking" [3].

These models might very likely follow the "laws of the visual brain" as Zeki has proposed. First, the law of constancy – seeking knowledge of the constant and essential properties of objects and surfaces; second, the law of abstraction – the process in which the particular is subordinated to the general, so that what is represented is applicable to many particulars; and third, the artistic demonstration of the process of abstraction: the reader may recall Kandinsky's "Composition VII" the creation of which evolved over thirty preparatory drawings, watercolors and oil studies.

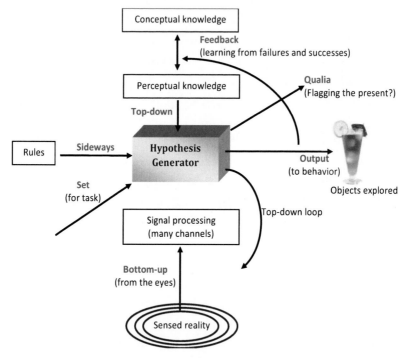

Figure 42. Hypothesis Generator, R. Gregory [2].

3. THE ARTISTIC PROCESS

The overall picture of the artistic process not only involves vision, but more importantly communication. The artist starts with his mind's eye image of the painting to be. Of course, this may be modified with time, trial and error. The picture, or artifact, is the message that acts as a channel of communication between the artist and the viewer. It is separate from either of them, in that it can be boxed and moved about from the time it is painted until the time that the viewer has an opportunity to see it. Finally, the viewer must have in his mind's eye a representation in order to perceive, see, and understand the picture. As an analytic demonstration of the relation between different pictorial representations [chosen by artist] and modes of AWE generated in the viewer during active looking (Figure 43).

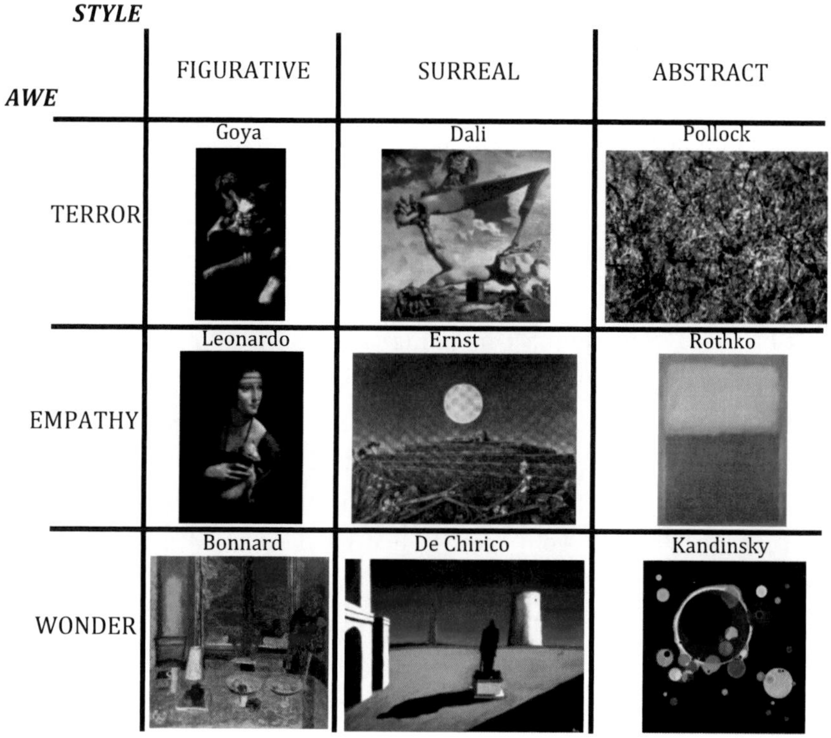

Figure 43. Example matrix of the AWE of the viewer to receive and to be stirred by the work of art as seen during different artistic "styles".

The entire process is driven by the passion of the artist to create and communicate, and the AWE of the viewer to receive and to be stirred by the work of art. There are many sub-processes that deserve individual consideration and that we have tried to put together in the previous chapters. The AWE of the viewer requires active vision in a top down mode: Silence around viewing is an indication of the profundity of the actively received communication. Of course, this example-matrix that we have selected is very subjective, and there may be thousands of choices for such a matrix. The point in this example is: The "AWE" – terror, empathy and wonder, – of the viewer/receiver in any case has to be an active process based on active looking with application of models initially private to the viewer, that eventually permit to recognize parts or the whole of the artist 's/sender 's model.

4. A PICTURE THAT IS NOT AN "ARTISTIC PICTURE"

There seems to be no word for a picture that is not an "artistic picture". The Italians use "quadro" (or rectangular or framed) for a painting but also "pittura" for a painting or a snapshot (in English, German, Italian, and Japanese). Japanese, perhaps, use a snapshot for a non-artistic picture. Stark has used "snapshot" vs "painting" and omitted "picture" (dictionary has a picture as a creative composition). Some have used "scene" (that can be decomposed into a number of designed, abstracted or composed separate pictures) for a non-painting picture. The term the "passing scene" may be better to illustrate a likely nonmentally created picture as an extension of the plain word "scene" that has been used in D. Chenyak's paper on scene analysis [4].

One could argue then that one cannot see non-internally-imagined pictures because in the instant of "seeing" it one constructs a hypothesized schema with wide-spread representation in the brain that gives it the quality of a picture that it shares with other pictures, especially art pictures. Therefore, the word "passing" to the word "scene" is added to indicate a set of visual signals not yet hypothesized by the brain: The word passing makes the scene very transient and less-attended to. Quantum theory states that the exact position and velocity-momentum of a particle cannot be both known simultaneously: as soon as you measure one variable the other becomes indistinct. Norbert Wiener expressed it as the fiction of a musical note in an exact instant of time and at an exact frequency. To establish an exact frequency one needs an infinite time series; to establish an exact instant one needs an infinite set of frequencies. He expressed it in the macro-physical world as "You can't play a jig on the low frequency pipes of an organ." An analogy between the scanpath theory and "quantum mechanics" is: As soon as one thinks – even intuitively – about a picture it becomes a mind's eye image with all the scanpath attributes: multiple cortical loci for the components of the image hypothesis and the Bayesian/probabilistic machinery. Thus before thinking or seeing a picture it has no mental representation; then immediately after thinking about it, it has such a representation!

5. THE PERCEPTUAL PROCESSES

The perceptual processes, hidden and historical in each of our brains remain incomplete senders and receivers: The words and their semantics, the sentences and their syntaxes. The paragraphs and their frames for an event, appear to be similarly available to several viewers. Science and humanities' aspects of art creation and viewing – and re-viewing – show the two sides of the same coin: art is a language, – but which language is used when communicating about art: iconic, natural, logical, mathematical? Which are the relationships between generally accepted ideas about art – humanities – and neuroscience relating to art? As we have seen, there are different aspects of visual art that influence the message between sender/artist and receiver/viewer: formal aspects of paintings as: perspective, sense of colors, line drawings, borderlines and overlay of things, contrasts, shading, formal hints towards other art/artists/times (cubist use of "primitive" sculpturing), etc. The content and/or the sum of differential contential parts of paintings are much harder to quantify than the formal ones, both in science and in humanities. Indirectly, eye movements and neuropsychological fMRI studies permit to gain some insight into the (multiple, dual) modes of control during artful picture viewing: but, they all have the disadvantage that they have to use very limited operationally defined experimental paradigms that relate very indirectly – if at all – to the content as a whole. Hints towards art history, philosophy, religion etc. lie therefore far outside of the possible perspective of such studies. Novelty, anticipations of the future, or antitheses are often hidden within paintings (Leonardo; Bonnard; Picasso): sociological/

historical context dependent features play an important role in this respect; aspects of information transfer itself: width, variance, robustness of information channels,

- Socio- biographical aspects of the artist and viewer, Mostly or often unknown to others: interactions between them, also provocations.
- General setting (museum, gallery, collection, atelier).
- Consequently, we can imagine some kind of multidimensional "space" where the above named parts are represented with information as the implicit variable:

Space (of the painting etc.), time (history, biographical time, presence and future) the "individual" [life] times of artist and viewer, types of languages, setting and set up of particular pictures, neuro-psychology/physiology/science of eye movements, attention and cognition.

6. WHY DO WE LOVE PICTURES AS WE LOVE NOVELS?

We are thus able to view a world, a novel – starkly black and white text – fixed and unalterable as the planets – several persons can share the identical world and then attempt to communicate about it, – and life – fluid – is defined in the novel only by irregular perceptual glimpse that anchor our billowing images – pictures. Several people with different perceptual samplings will forever have difficulty communicate about it. But in a larger sense as we read – read the picture – there are two perceptual and imagined worlds, the writer's/artist's and the reader's/viewer's that are reaching out to communicate.

The text itself is a coded message accessible only to the privileged sender and receiver. The lower levels of the artifact, the words and their semantics, the sentences and their syntaxes, the paragraphs and their frames for an event, appear to be similarly available to several readers. Yet each of us can paraphrase or interpret uniquely much as we do in the so-called "real" world. To paraphrase is to capture a text in our own words, with our own semantics and syntax, with our own organization of smaller and larger events.

In what ways is a painting similar and in what ways different? There is the coded message, the beautiful and skillfully contrived artifact exposed completely in its frame. Yet the same barriers to communication are here. What is the code? What is the message? From what culture came this sight? The perceptual processes, hidden and historical in each of our brains remain incomplete to senders and receivers. The Picture itself is a coded message accessible only to the privileged sender and receiver. The lower levels of the artifact, the real/abstract details of the picture and their relations, their organization and structure within the picture, the larger parts of the picture and their "weight" compared to each other and altogether: all appear to be similarly available to several viewers.

Since an image is the "imitation of the object's external form", the image represents, in the sense of: *calling up before the mind or senses, by description or portrayal or imagination, figure, place, likeness of.* What it thus stands for, is a specimen of, that fills the place of, is a substitute for. Perhaps there is more to this formula than meets the eye. Then there is that age-old problem of universals as applied to art. It has received its classical formulation in the Platonizing theories of the Academicians (Gombrich [5]). The story line of a novel, a segment of time, becomes a plot when it embeds a cause and effect. Not as in real life, in the novel each event must have a cause and effect, as it was created in the writer's mind and on the writer's computer keyboard. We can seize that assurance. Motivation, character, circumstances, history all contrive to yield the events in our fictional causal world, whereas in our real world also non causal parts maybe subjectively implied by us – although the physical/biological world always implies causes that we are not always able to detect.

REFERENCES

[1] S. Zeki, "Artistic creativity and the brain.," *Science,*, vol. 293, p. 51–52., 2001.

[2] R. Gregory, *Even odder perceptions*. New York London, 1994.

[3] S. Hustvedt, *Mysteries of the rectangle*. Princeton.: Architectural press, 2005.

[4] D. A. Chernyak and L. W. Stark, "Top-down guided eye movements," *IEEE Trans. Syst. Man, Cybern. Part B Cybern.*, vol. 31, no. 4, pp. 514–522, 2001.

[5] E. H. Gombrich, *Art and Illusion: A study in the psychology of pictorial presentation*. London: Phaidon, 1968.

INDEX